THE
*Pleasure*
of Your
Company

SIMPLE IDEAS *for*
ENJOYABLE ENTERTAINING

SUSAN WALES AND ANN PLATZ

ILLUSTRATIONS BY
KATHRYN ANDREWS FINCHER

HARVEST HOUSE PUBLISHERS
EUGENE, OREGON 97402

*The Pleasure of Your Company*

Copyright © 1999 by Susan Wales and Ann Platz
Published by Harvest House Publishers
Eugene, Oregon 97402

**Library of Congress Cataloging-in-Publication Data**

Platz, Ann.

The pleasure of your company / Ann Platz and Susan Wales ; artwork
by Kathryn Andrews Fincher

    p.    cm.

    ISBN 0-7369-0111-6

    1. Entertaining.    2. Menus.    3.Cookery.    I. Wales, Susan.

II. Title.

TX731.P57    1999

642' .4--dc21

99-18437

CIP

Artwork designs are reproduced under license from Arts Uniq', Inc., Cookeville, TN
and may not be reproduced without permission. For information regarding art prints
featured in this book, please contact:

Arts Uniq'
P.O. Box 3085
Cookeville, TN 38502
1.800.223.5020

Design and production by Koechel Peterson & Associates
Minneapolis, Minnesota

Harvest House Publishers has made every effort to trace the ownership of all poems
and quotes. In the event of a question arising from the use of a poem or quote, we
regret any error made and will be pleased to make the necessary correction in future
editions of this book.

**Printed in Hong Kong.**

00 01 02 03 04 05 06 07 08    / IM /    10 9 8 7 6 5 4 3

# Contents

# It's Not What You Do, But How You Do It

When we do the *best* we can,
We never know what *miracle* is wrought in our life,
Or in the *life* of another.

HELEN KELLER

*"The Pleasure of Your Company."* It's a lovely phrase, isn't it? It conjures up images of warm hospitality and tantalizingly good food, of friends and family, of formal starched linen napkins and informal red-and-white tablecloths, of picnics and lunches, of eggnog and cold lemonade, and of memories and those moments yet to be made.

We are social creatures who want to surround ourselves with those things that matter most in our lives: friends, family, laughter, and love. So why does the mere thought of entertaining strike terror in most of us? Perhaps we have become discouraged as we've flipped through hundreds of magazines or watched famous hostesses prepare an omelet or concoct a sauce that made brain surgery look easy. We are overwhelmed by the thought of it all, or maybe we are afraid we'll do something wrong.

We are Ann Platz (a decorator) and Susan Wales (a party-planner), here to join you every step of the way of your entertaining journey. Heirs of legendary Southern hospitality, we were taught by our mothers, grandmothers, and aunts to entertain at the drop of a hat with ease and elegance. We invite you to benefit from our "rearing" as we describe our unique party ideas and favorite recipes.

I (Ann) come from a long line of renowned South Carolina hostesses, beginning over 200 years ago with Rebecca Brewton Motte. During the

Revolutionary War, she was evicted from her house by British soldiers who took it over as their headquarters. Rather than allow the Red Coats to occupy her home, Rebecca ordered her servants to shoot flaming arrows onto the roof, burning her house to the ground.

Not long after the British conceded to the Colonists, Rebecca invited both the American and British officers to dine on her lawn as her home smoldered in the background. Now that's entertaining against all odds!

Together in *The Pleasure of Your Company* we will be your innovative guides to easy and effortless entertaining. We want you to discover the kind of entertaining that makes you feel most comfortable, whether it be formal or informal, tons of people or simply an intimate gathering of close friends.

We have assembled some of our favorite party ideas for brunches and lunches, picnics and barbecues, dinner parties and special occasions to help you create memorable holiday gatherings and extra-special moments.

Remember, this is entertaining for the *everywoman*. You don't have to be the greatest hostess to ever tie on an apron. You just have to *look* the part. The best hostesses know the hidden secrets. We are going to share them with you. Effortless entertaining allows you to enjoy your party, delight in your guests, and savor some delicious food. Hosting should be about breathing and laughing and learning to deal with the minor mishaps that will inevitably come your way.

Years ago, when I (Susan) was a co-hostess at a bridal luncheon, I was loading casseroles I had spent hours preparing into the back of my car. When I returned with the second box, to my horror, my neighbor's two large afghan hounds were on their hind legs at the back of my car. Despite my screams, those dogs polished off enough casserole for thirty people in thirty seconds flat.

What's a hostess to do—the luncheon was scheduled to begin in an hour and there was not enough food left for the guests! With no time to panic, I rushed to the supermarket, bought some cooked chicken, several cans of soup, and some crackers. In less than twenty minutes, I had put together a couple of delicious casseroles that received rave reviews!

My *dog* experience teaches several essential lessons about entertaining. First the obvious: Never leave food within reach of a dog. Second, you can always find a solution to any mishap. And, most importantly, you can serve quick and easy dishes that are just as tasty as the more complicated ones.

A favorite story of mine (Ann) involved my sister, Mary Ashley Gardner. When she and her husband joined a dinner group, she was determined to entertain with style. Mary Ashley scoured magazines and cookbooks searching for the most unique dessert recipe, and finally settled on a fancy chocolate cake for dessert.

A few hours before her guests were to arrive, Mary Ashley looked with pride on her delectable dessert. It was perfect. Thrilled at her obvious success, she accidentally slammed the oven door. As we said before, usually everything is redeemable with a little imagination, but peeking inside the oven, my sister could not fathom a way to save her dessert, so she phoned her 911-Friend-Who-Knows-How-To-Cook.

"Go to the store and buy Cool Whip® and two graham cracker crusts," her friend advised, "they will fix any dessert disaster."

So Mary Ashley mixed this strange brownish concoction with Cool Whip®, dumped it into her store-bought graham cracker crusts, and put them in the freezer for twenty minutes. The dessert was superb and all of her guests prodded her for the secret ingredients. My sister simply smiled and announced that her "Sunken Chocolate Pie" was an old family recipe!

The key to being a successful hostess is not what you do, but how you do it. If you can read, you can cook. And, if you will read *The Pleasure of Your Company*, you can entertain. This is our promise to you.

# 1
# Easy Entertaining

Let brotherly *love* continue.
Be not forgetful to entertain strangers:
for thereby some have entertained *angels* unawares.

THE BOOK OF HEBREWS

*W*elcome to the joys of entertaining! You are about to embark on a journey to more abundant living. Entertaining is a happy celebration of life, family, and friends. Inviting a guest into your home is one of the highest honors you can bestow upon an individual. Whether it's a cup of coffee with a friend or a formal dinner for twelve, your hospitality is always a gift to others.

There is no greater joy than gathering your family around the table to share not just the meal, but also the events of the day. Celebrate the holidays with special touches by creating a festive atmosphere at meal time. To create memories and traditions, make a heart-shaped piece of toast for breakfast on Valentine's Day, tuck a shamrock sandwich in a lunch box on St. Patrick's Day, and add a candle to pancakes for birthdays. Involve your entire family in making every day special and your children will inherit your gift of hospitality.

Entertaining doesn't have to be difficult. It can be done by anyone, anywhere, and on any budget! We'll show you how to make up for any lack in resources with a little imagination. *The Pleasure of Your Company* presents fresh, new, and simple ideas to spark and inspire creativity, especially for those individuals who are novices in this area.

Even skeptics will soon discover that entertaining today can be effortless if you follow the simple suggestions, menus, and party themes outlined in our book! You will learn that you can be a charming hostess without spending a lot of time, effort, and money.

# Tips on How to Entertain

There *is* nothing that can *light*
up a room like a *joyous* hostess.

SUSAN WALES

## Plan! Plan! Plan!

How do you begin? An architect would never dream of designing without a set of plans, and the same is true when having a party. First of all, choose a date and select your party theme. Setting a theme will not only give you a plan of action, it also creates an air of excitement among your guests. Next, compile your guest list. Remember that the best parties have the most interesting mix of people.

Now choose your decor and your menu or use one of the menus we have provided. Make your grocery list and an inventory list of the items you will need such as linens, dishes, and serving pieces. Launch a plan of attack for house cleaning. It's as simple as that!

## Invitations

It is perfectly acceptable to invite your guests by telephone unless it's a formal party. If you are planning a theme party, sending invitations will create anticipation for the event. Invitations can be purchased, designed, or handwritten. There are hundreds of clever invitations that you can purchase, but we have provided several ideas if you prefer to do your own.

## Setting the Stage
### LIGHTING

What woman doesn't look more beautiful in candlelight? Use candles everywhere. Did you know that if you store your candles in the refrigerator prior to using, this will prevent the wax from dripping?

Dimmers on the lights in your dining room and entertaining areas provide wonderful lighting options. Light your candles and then turn the dimmer down to match the color of the light from the candles for a beautiful ambiance. For a romantic evening, replace regular light bulbs with pink light bulbs to cast a soft glow.

For outdoor lighting hang strands of twinkling lights to line walks, lamp posts, walls, and trees. Use yellow light bulbs in your outdoor fixtures and citronella candles to discourage insects. You can also use hurricane lights, tiki torches, and luminarias (paper bags with votive candles nested in sand).

## FRAGRANCE

If the weather is cool, light a roaring fire to welcome your guests and create a cozy atmosphere. Purchase copper sulfate from your druggist and sprinkle it in the fireplace for colorful flames that cast a lovely hue on the room. Toss a mixture of orange and lemon peels with cinnamon sticks and cloves into the fire for a spicy aroma that will float through your party. This is a particularly romantic setting for you and your husband alone!

The aroma of oranges spiked with cloves and cinnamon boiling in apple cider on the stove or a fresh loaf of bread baking in the oven will awaken your guests' senses like nothing else! Scented candles throughout the entertaining area will add a special ambiance. Light bulb rings with one or two drops of your favorite potpourri oil will effortlessly fill the room with a lovely scent.

## MUSIC

There's nothing like music to liven up or lend a touch of romance to a special occasion. Usually a collection played on your stereo is all you'll need. Make long-playing tapes, or if you have a disc-changer, fill it with soft background selections. Classical selections are especially nice for a seated dinner party. Remember that your music should never be at a level that interferes with party conversation. If you hire a live musical group for your party, always audition them first.

## FLOWERS

Simplicity is the key to your table decorations and these helpful hints will inspire your own ideas for your next party. Whatever the occasion, the centerpiece should mirror the event. Always make sure that flower fragrance doesn't overpower your food and that the centerpiece is low enough so that your guests can see one another. You can float a single blossom—a camellia, a magnolia, or a hydrangea in a beautiful crystal bowl for a simple, but elegant, centerpiece.

The more formal the party, the more formal the flowers and the container will be. Explore your house for imaginative containers. You can cover tin cans with fabric or greenery or use a teapot, a basket, or a hat! Some hostesses display collections of porcelain, teacups, or sea shells to accent their table. The possibilities are endless.

For a special touch, arrange a centerpiece with fruit or vegetables mixed with greenery or flowers. Try lemons, limes, apples, and oranges polished with cooking oil. I (Susan) often fill a flower container with lemons, cranberries, or apples for color and also to hold the flowers in place. Scooped-out pumpkins, cabbages, squashes, oranges, artichokes, melons, and other fruits and vegetables all make charming containers for flowers and votive candles.

Bedded plants such as geraniums or pansies in a basket add a nice touch for some occasions. You can present your guests with a flower at the end of the evening or plant them in your garden.

*He that has a merry heart hath a continual feast.*

THE BOOK OF PROVERBS

## FOOD

If you are just starting out, the best advice we can give you is to keep it simple. Always plan a menu you can do ahead or where at least the majority of the dishes can be made ahead. Even those who are uncertain about cooking should not be discouraged from entertaining. You can purchase any of your food items pre-cooked.

An essential tool for any would-be hostess is a good basic cookbook. You will find recipes for most of the food contained in our book in a cookbook, but we have also provided some of our own recipes, many of which Susan has created, that are quick, easy, and delicious. Check to see what seasonal vegetables are available, always use the freshest food and, if you are planning on serving a particular cut of meat or fish, order it in advance from your butcher.

With all the wonderful prepared foods that are available today, you can serve a feast using just the microwave and your oven. Lasagna for a large crowd that even rivals my homemade recipe can be found in the frozen food section! Just add a salad and some garlic bread.

If you buy food that is already prepared, add your own personal signature to the dish by adding spices, fresh herbs, or a dressing or sauce. One of my (Susan's) favorite recipes featured in this book is my cranberry chicken salad. I always buy the chicken salad at the deli, add my special ingredients, and make my own dressing. My guests rave over this delicious dish that takes only minutes to make and the results are fabulous.

A smart hostess always keeps items on hand such as pasta, bottled sauces, and eggs. These are things that cook in minutes. There are delicious frozen pies and quiches that you can purchase and store in your freezer for emergencies. These items really come in handy if you run out of food on your buffet table or if you burn the roast at the last minute. If all else fails, you can call for pizza delivery! With a little kitchen savvy and a great sense of humor, you can overcome any obstacle that stands in the way of entertaining.

# Serving

There are various ways to serve your meal to your guests:

## BUFFET

The most popular way to serve at a party, especially for a small space, is buffet. The hostess arranges the buffet table with the food and stacks plates at the beginning of the buffet. Place your silverware, napkins, and beverages at the end to allow your guests to keep their hands free to serve themselves.

## SERVICE

The guests are seated and the hostess or a server serves the plates at the table or serves the plates in the kitchen and brings them to the table.

## FAMILY STYLE

The food is placed on the table and passed to the seated guests.

If you don't have enough dishes and serving pieces, use plastic cups and pretty paper plates and napkins. Vegetables, fruits, and breads also make great containers for food. Serve soup in bread bowls, sorbet in a melon or pineapple boat, and chili in a pumpkin. Put a paper or linen liner in a basket to serve bread, corn-on-the-cob, or baked potatoes. Another solution is to ask a friend to co-host a party with you and pool your resources and your serving pieces! For extra space to keep items cold and drinks on ice, bring in ice chests.

Once the cooking is done, the manner in which you serve the food is an artistic opportunity. Use simple garnishes to dress up the serving plate. If you are artistic and want to experiment with fancy garnishes, there are several good books available. Beautiful and inexpensive garnishes that would take hours to make can often be found in the deli of your local grocery store. For simple garnishes, put a circle of rosemary around a chicken on a platter or lemon slices around asparagus or kumquats and bay leaves around a turkey. A pork tenderloin at the holidays can be garnished with alternating slices of green and red apples with parsley. A cake or pie looks pretty with flowers or frosted grapes.

## The Most Important Ingredient

Congratulations! You have just graduated a crash course in entertaining, and now we will reveal the most important ingredient. Being a successful hostess doesn't depend on the external—the beautifully decorated home, the priceless china, the gourmet food. It depends on what is inside you—your joy, caring, and warmth. The hostess who makes her guests feel welcome, special, and loved will remain in the hearts of her guests forever, long after the memories of the evening have grown dim.

*The Pleasure of Your Company* was written to inspire you to draw upon your own strength, personal style, and unique talents as you open your home and your heart to others. Each one of us is unique, and we all have our own special gifts that make us who we are. There's a seed of creativity planted in all of us that needs to be nurtured. Instead of comparing yourself to someone more creative, build on their knowledge to unwrap the gifts in you.

With *The Pleasure of Your Company* as your guide, and your own special touches, each guest who visits your home will leave with a little piece of your heart. It's time to begin your great adventure into the world of brunches, lunches, barbecues, picnics, dinners, parties, and holiday celebrations. Remember, we'll be right by your side!

> Do not be overly concerned with the *interior*
> of your home, it's the *inside* of your *heart*
> that your *guests* will remember.
>
> ANN PLATZ

# 2
## Brunches

There's nothing *like* the aroma of home-cooking
*to* bring your *loved* ones together.
SUSAN WALES

*A* cross between breakfast and lunch, the brunch is a delightful way to entertain today! Prepare a bountiful feast of morning fare to tempt your guests: ham, eggs, bacon, seafood, grits, salads, assorted breads, fruits, coffee, and delectable desserts. A brunch is the perfect solution for everyone's busy lifestyle…your guests can arrive at their leisure around 10:00 A.M., enjoy the fun, food, and fellowship, and then have the rest of their day free!

It has become a popular custom to invite guests to enjoy a hearty midmorning buffet in anticipation of a special day's events (perhaps a sporting event or wedding). A Bachelor Brunch is the perfect solution for entertaining the bridegroom before the ceremony while the bride and her attendants indulge in a morning of relaxation and pampering.

Following a momentous occasion, a brunch not only adds a happy ending, it also allows your guests to discuss the exciting details of the night before! But you don't need a special occasion. Invite your friends for brunch after church.

Greet your guests with a steaming cup of coffee. For a breakfast or brunch, we recommend setting up a coffee bar with regular and decaffeinated coffee, sugar, artificial sweeteners, half and half, cream, non-fat milk, and a variety of the flavored non-dairy creamers. Also provide shakers of chocolate, cinnamon, vanilla sugar, and nutmeg for a special treat.

# Baby Shower Brunch

*People* are either born *hosts*
or born *guests.*

Sir Max Beerbohm

This creative brunch usually honors the mother-to-be, but recently we entertained a prospective grandmother who was unable to attend her daughter's baby shower in a distant city. We honored our friend with a Grandmother Shower. Take lots of pictures so the honoree can share the event with her family.

## Invitations

You can purchase your invitations or write invitations on white or ivory stationery with a child's hand prints drawn in blue and pink. A simpler way is to write the invitations on pink and blue stationery with a pen of the opposite color.

> ## It's a Grandmother Shower
> Honoring
> Marie Alderson
> Brunch
> Date, Time, Place
> Hostess
> RSVP: Telephone Number    Attire: Casual

## Decorations

Spread your dining room table with a white cloth overlaid with tulle that can be purchased inexpensively at a fabric store. Bunch the tulle at each corner and tie with pink and blue ribbons. Decorate a playpen, porta-crib, or large baby carriage with ribbons and balloons to hold all the presents. (Grandmother-appropriate presents are photo albums, picture frames, bibs, a silver baby cup, porta-crib, stroller, books, and toys.)

18

## Flowers

For a spectacular main centerpiece, fill a doll stroller with a large bouquet of pink roses, white lilies, blue hydrangeas, and greenery with streamers of blue, pink, and white ribbon. For centerpieces at smaller tables, fill baby bottles with miniature pink roses and colored streamers. When the party's over, send the baby bottles to the mother-to-be.

## Place Cards and Name Tags

Using a colored marker, personalize small baby rattles with each guest's name to use as place cards. Pin name tags on each guest with blue or pink diaper pins.

## Music

Select some tapes of lullabies to play softly in the background interspersed with children nursery rhyme songs.

# Menu

Coffee Bar, Hot Tea, Juice

Chilled Lime Gazpacho

Quiche Lorraine

Spinach Salad

Hot Curried Fruit

Blue and Pink Petits Fours Trimmed with Rattles

# CHILLED LIME GAZPACHO

*Serves 4-6*

Blend the following in a blender:

3 large, ripe tomatoes

1 cup each of coarsely chopped:
bell pepper, cucumber, and onion

1 clove garlic

1/2 cup each fresh chives and parsley
(or cilantro)

1/4 cup dill

1/2 cup olive oil

1/2 cup lime juice

3 cups beef or chicken stock

Refrigerate for two hours. Serve in a frosted mug or bowl and garnish with a dollop of sour cream and chopped chives or dill.

# HOT CURRIED FRUIT

*Serves 12*

1 16-ounce can peaches

1 16-ounce can pear halves

1 16-ounce can pineapple chunks

1 16-ounce can apricot halves

12 maraschino cherries

1/3 cup butter

1 cup brown sugar

4 teaspoons curry powder

Drain fruit and place in a round, oven-proof dish or a 9 x 13 casserole dish. Melt butter in a sauce pan, add sugar and curry powder. Pour butter mixture over fruit and bake at 325° for 30 minutes. This is a dish that can be made ahead and refrigerated. Heat just prior to serving.

*Love* is a fruit in *season*
at all *times.*
MOTHER TERESA

# Sunday Birdhouse Brunch

*Joy* cometh
in the *morning*.
<small>THE BOOK OF PSALMS</small>

Invite your family and friends to drop by after church for Sunday Brunch to celebrate a special occasion or just to get together and have fun! The following brunch is centered around a birdhouse theme and can be made ahead.

## Invitations

For a casual event, you can invite your guests by phone or you can send written invitations in birdhouse shapes.

> ### Birds of a Feather
> ### Are Flocking Together
> For Brunch
> At Jan and Tom Linder's Home
> Drop by after church on Sunday, Date
> at 12:30 P.M.
> RSVP: Telephone Number   Attire: Sunday Best

## Decorations and Flowers

Attach birds to a wreath on the front door. A collection of bird houses makes a delightful centerpiece. Tuck sprigs of greenery or flowers into the opening of the houses. Hang a bird feeder outside the window and watch the birds enjoy lunch, too!

## Place Cards and Name Tags

If guests are seated, mark each place with a miniature bird nest purchased at a craft store. Attach bird stickers or bird feathers to name tags.

Play your favorite church hymns or songbird tapes.

*~ Menu ~*

*Ham and Biscuits*
*Savory Sausage Ring with Eggs*
*Potatoes and Onions*
*Vegetables with Dip*
*Brownies and Lemon Squares*

## SAVORY SAUSAGE RING WITH EGGS

$1^1/2$ pounds bulk pork sausage

$3/4$ cup uncooked oatmeal

$2/3$ cup chopped peeled apple

$2/3$ cup milk

$3/4$ teaspoon salt

$3/4$ teaspoon crushed basil

$1/2$ teaspoon sage

$1/2$ cup chopped onion

7 large eggs

1 16-ounce can peach halves

Beat 1 egg with milk and combine with sausage, oats, apple, salt, onion, basil, and sage. Mix thoroughly. Drain peaches and place peach halves, cavity side up, in the bottom of an ungreased 6-cup ring mold. Spoon sausage mixture over and between peaches, packing it firmly into mold. Bake in oven at 350° for one hour. Invert mold on shallow pan lined with absorbent paper. Do not remove mold. Let stand until grease drains off. Scramble remaining 6 eggs. Turn sausage ring right side up and invert onto serving plate. Place scrambled eggs in the center of ring and serve hot.

# Golf or Tennis Brunch

The Golf or Tennis Brunch is an excellent way to gather fans before attending a tournament or watching a televised event. Celebrate a job promotion or a birthday with this sporty party.

## Invitations

These invitations were designed for either a golfing husband's birthday party or a ladies' tennis brunch. Both can be written on bright green stationery or design your own in the shape of a ball.

### It's a Hole in Fun...
### at the Johnsons'

Come putter around at Brunch
Honoring Bruce Johnson's 40th Birthday
We'll Tee-Off on Date at 10:00 A.M.

Patty Johnson

RSVP: Telephone Number     Dress: Golfing Attire

### Love Forty!

Leave your rackets behind, be as quiet as a mouse
Bounce on over to Vickie Ford's house
For a Surprise 40th Birthday Brunch
Honoring Nancy Huey
Date at 10:00 A.M.

RSVP: Telephone     Dress: Tennis Attire

## Decorations and Flowers (Golf)

For the centerpiece, design a putting green with moss and sand and arrange with flowers and a fortieth hole. If you don't have a green tablecloth, purchase a green paper cloth or inexpensive disposable green vinyl cloth. Display golf clubs in a corner and shine a spotlight on them.

## Place Cards and Name Tags

Use scorecards for your place cards and glue golf tees to the name tags.

## Decorations and Flowers (Tennis)

Use a green cloth on the table that you can outline in white masking tape to resemble a court. For flowers use large yellow mums and greenery in a vase or buy a round topiary form and secure it in a clay pot. Cover base of topiary with green moss and attach miniature yellow mums with florist pins or glue to the top. Glue white mum petals to make seams on the tennis ball. For a door decoration, cross two tennis rackets and weave a nosegay of flowers on the strings with streamers or glue tennis balls to a wreath form.

## Place Cards and Name Tags

Mark each guest's place with a personalized tennis ball. Make name tags in the shape of tennis balls.

## Music

Choose music that is a favorite of the guest of honor to play softly in the background.

## Menu

Orange Juice and Coffee Bar
Hot Crab Dip with Chips and Veggies
Hole-in-One or Tennis-Ball
Toast with Egg
Cheese Grits
Bacon, Sausage Links, or Baked Ham
Hot Cinnamon Fruit Served in Scalloped Orange Shells
Sticky Buns and Assorted Muffins
Mold Ice Cream Balls and Roll in Coconut to Resemble Golf Balls or Lemon
Sherbet or Sorbet to Resemble Tennis Balls and Serve with Cookies or
Birthday Cake in the Shape of a Tennis Racket, Tennis Court, or 18th Green

# HOLE-IN-ONE TOAST WITH EGG

2 tablespoons butter        Egg

Toast

Use a round cookie cutter and cut circle out of bread. Break the egg and drop the egg into the hole. Fry the egg in 2 tablespoons butter or margarine over medium heat on both sides until done and serve hot.

# HOT CINNAMON FRUIT IN SCALLOPED ORANGE SHELLS

*Serves 6*

3 large oranges

1 16-ounce can fruit cocktail, drained

1/2 tablespoon cinnamon

1/2 teaspoon nutmeg

1 teaspoon allspice

1/4 cup butter

Cut oranges in half. Remove the fruit from the shells and use to make orange juice. Scallop top of orange shell, if desired. Set aside. Melt butter in a saucepan. Add spices and stir well. Add fruit cocktail and heat until warm. Pour into orange shells and serve hot. Can be served in custard dishes instead of orange shells.

Cooking *may* be as *much* a means
of self-expression as *any* of the arts.

FANNIE MERRITT FARMER

# 3

*Luncheons*

My home is a *treasure* chest
In which I collect *memories*
Of my *family* and friends.

<small>CLARA FERREE SMITH</small>

*L*uncheons are our favorite way of entertaining for *just the girls!* There's always an occasion to celebrate this midday meal. Luncheons usually last from 12:00 until 3:00 P.M. It is much more fun when your luncheon can be focused on an honoree…a friend's birthday, a bride, an expectant mother, or an out-of-town guest.

Six to twelve women is the ideal size for a luncheon. Card tables with crisp white cloths can be set up for extra space. Prepare a luncheon of three or four light courses. Dainty sandwiches, cheese straws, delectable salads, and exquisite but light desserts will delight your friends.

You should plan an attractive presentation for your feminine guests, so bring out the china, the crystal, and the silver. Creative place cards such as a flower pot with the guest's name or a tiny box filled with a special verse can also serve as favors. At one party we used recipe cards for place cards for our guests to take home.

You can seat your guests at the dining room table or take them out to the terrace or the garden on a sunny day. Let your surroundings work for you when planning the decor and the menu! We once seated guests next to Susan's rose garden and not only used roses for the centerpieces, but also wrote a poem about a rose on each guest's place card and used rosebuds to garnish the dessert plate. It was charming!

With today's busy lives and schedules, entertaining with a luncheon has become a rarity, so make this special occasion memorable in every way!

# A Garden Party

This is a wonderful luncheon to honor a bride, a birthday, welcome spring, or for no occasion at all. It's an easy party to prepare for, but the results are spectacular. Spring is bursting out all over!

## Invitations

Paste your invitations on the back of seed packets of summer flowers.

## Merry, Merry

How does Ann's Garden Grow?
Come to a Spring Luncheon
Ann Platz's Patio
Date at 12:00 Noon
RSVP: Telephone     Dress: Casual

## Decorations and Flowers

Serve your guests buffet style. Cover the serving table or counter with moss available at a garden store or florist. At the home supply store, purchase a short picket fence (the kind used to border flowers) and insert into moss.

Tie 10"-12" sunflowers with raffia onto the picket fence and label each flower with a seed packet to identify each of the salad fixings. Assemble a large bowl of salad greens and clay pots to hold all the salad fixings. Place small garden trowels in clay dishes in front of the pots to serve the items from them. Use small watering cans for an assortment of salad dressings. Put rolls in a large basket behind the fence. If your party is for a birthday or shower, use a large wheelbarrow to hold the gifts.

## Place Cards and Name Tags

Tie a daisy on a pretty floral napkin with raffia or ribbon. Take miniature clay pots approximately 2" in diameter, and plant with spring flowers to double as place cards and table decorations. With a colorful marker write the person's name on their flower pot and give it as a party favor.

*Music*

Play Vivaldi's *Seasons* concerto, "Spring," softly in the background.

## *Menu*

*Grilled Chicken or Shrimp with Tossed Salad and Dressing*
*Tomatoes    Celery*
*Carrots    Assorted Beans*
*Miniature Corn    Sunflower Seeds*
*Peppers    Radishes*
*Cucumbers    Squash*
*Garlic Rolls    Pecan Tassies*
*Iced Tea with Mint*

## PECAN TASSIES

| | |
|---|---|
| 1  3-ounce package cream cheese | $1/4$ teaspoon salt |
| 1  cup sifted plain flour | 1  cup pecans |
| $1/2$  cup margarine | |

Cream the first four ingredients together and refrigerate for one hour. Roll into 2 dozen 1" balls and mash into tiny muffin tins. Mash half of chopped nuts into dough. Use other half of nuts for filling below.

### FILLING:

| | |
|---|---|
| 1  egg | 1  teaspoon vanilla |
| $3/4$  cup light brown sugar | $1/8$  teaspoon salt |
| 1  tablespoon soft margarine | |

Mix all ingredients together with pecans and fill shells. Bake at 350° for 15 minutes. Reduce heat to 250° until filling is set or until a knife inserted in the filling comes out clean.

# Lunch and Learn Basket Lunch

*I know I'm home by the fragrance*
*of my mother's kitchen.*

SUSAN WALES

Women's lives have changed and ladies' luncheons aren't as prevalent as they once were. With so many career women, volunteers, and mothers with small children, there's rarely time to sit down and enjoy lunch with your lady friends.

An excellent way to get your friends together is to offer them an opportunity to attend a Bible Study, hear a speaker, or enjoy a performer. Working women and busy mothers will often take time out of their day to join you for this occasion. Provide a basket or box lunch for them to hold in their lap while they enjoy the speaker or entertainment.

## Invitations

Make your invitations in the shape of a basket or draw a basket on colored paper.

Lunch and Learn
How to Encourage Your Kids
Dr. Charles Moore, UCLA Pediatric Psychiatrist
A TISKET, A TASKET
LUNCH IS IN THE BASKET
Martha Wolfe's
Date at 12:00 P.M.
RSVP: Telephone Number     Dress: Casual

## Decorations and Flowers

This party is very simply done. Place an arrangement of flowers in a basket on the dining room table. Prepare luncheon baskets ahead of time. Line the baskets with pretty white doilies or paper place mats. Tuck in a floral paper napkin and attach a fresh flower with a colorful ribbon to the handle.

## Place Cards and Name Tags

Each woman's name can be attached to the handle of her basket with twist tags.

## Music

Since there is a lecturer, only play music at the beginning of the gathering until the ladies take their seats. Use a soft classical selection.

## Menu

Cranberry Chicken Salad Croissants

Vegetable Sticks Tied with Raffia

Asparagus, Carrots, and Celery

Apple with Congo Bars

## CRANBERRY CHICKEN SALAD CROISSANTS

| | |
|---|---|
| 4 cups cooked chicken | 1 cup Craisins™ |
| 1/2 cup chopped celery | 1/2 cup chopped pecans |
| 1/2 cup chopped purple onion | 1/2 cup mayonnaise |
| | 1 teaspoon lemon juice |

Mix together all ingredients and serve on croissants. Drizzle with cranberry dressing.

## CRANBERRY DRESSING

| | |
|---|---|
| 3/4 cup salad oil | 1 teaspoon salt |
| 1/4 cup vinegar | 1 teaspoon sugar |
| 1 cup whole canned cranberries | 1/2 teaspoon paprika |

Blend ingredients in a blender. For easier dressing, combine a bottle of Italian dressing with a 16-ounce can of whole cranberries. You will have extra dressing left over.

# CONGO BARS

*4 dozen*

1  16-ounce box light brown sugar
<sup></sup>

1/2 cup butter, melted

3  eggs

2  cups all-purpose flour, sifted

2  teaspoons baking powder

1  teaspoon vanilla

   Pinch of salt

1  cup chopped nuts

1  12-ounce package of chocolate
   morsels

Combine sugar with butter and stir. Beat in eggs one at a time. Fold in flour that has been sifted with baking powder and a pinch of salt. Add vanilla, nuts, and chocolate morsels. Pour into a 9 x 13 greased pan. Bake at 325° for 25 minutes. Cool. Cut into squares.

It's food too *fine* for *angels,*
yet come, take and eat thy fill!
It's *Heaven's* sugar *cake.*

Edward Taylor

# Mad Hatter Luncheon

*No **effort** that we make to attain*
*something **beautiful** is ever lost.*

HELEN KELLER

This is a very feminine ladies' luncheon appropriate for a bridal shower, birthday party, or just for fun! Greet your guests with a tray of pink lemonade. I (Susan) hosted this party as a shower for a bride and everyone wore a hat, brought antique linens, and recited their favorite love poem to the bride-to-be. Ann honored a friend's birthday and the guests each brought a tea cup reflecting their personality to replace a collection her friend had lost. Use your own creative ideas to honor your friends and family.

## Invitations

Send the invitations on hot pink hats.

Eliza MacLemore and Margaret McClatchey
request the pleasure of your company in your finest hat
### At a Linen Shower Luncheon
Honoring Margo Cloer
Bring a love poem for the bride-to-be
Date at 12:00 Noon
Address
RSVP: Telephone          Dress: Party Dress

## Decorations, Name Tags, and Place Cards

It's fun to be a female and this is a luncheon where you celebrate all that's feminine with pink as the theme! The table is set with a white cloth, crystal, china, and silver. Flowers attached to the brim of a hat with a ribbon makes a wonderful centerpiece. You can also invert a hat and put a bouquet inside. Scatter rose petals around the centerpiece. Attach rosebuds to heart-shaped place cards. Use heart-shaped name tags. Invert an umbrella decorated with streamers and fill it with presents.

Shrimp Salad on Lettuce
Tomato Aspic
Cheese Straws
Heart-Shaped Meringues with Strawberries

## TOMATO ASPIC

| | |
|---|---|
| 1 envelope lemon gelatin | 1 cup chopped celery |
| 1/4 cup cold water | 1/2 cup chopped green olives |
| 1 10 1/2-ounce can tomato soup | 1 teaspoon finely chopped onion |
| 3 ounces cream cheese | 1/2 pound cooked shrimp (optional) |

Dissolve gelatin in cold water. Dissolve cream cheese in hot soup and add gelatin. To this stir in celery, olives, and onion. Place shrimp in the mixture without additional stirring. Salt to taste. Place in individual greased molds or into a quart ring mold. Refrigerate until firm.

## HEART-SHAPED MERINGUES WITH STRAWBERRIES

*1 dozen meringues*
*Preheat oven to 225°*

| | |
|---|---|
| 4 large egg whites | 1 quart of sliced fresh strawberries |
| 1 cup sugar | Vanilla Ice cream |

Line 2 baking sheets with foil; butter foil. Place a 3 3/4" heart-shaped cookie cutter on foil-lined sheet. Using an electric mixer, beat whites in large bowl to soft peaks. Gradually add 1 cup sugar; continuing beating until stiff and shiny. Spoon 1/4 cup meringue inside cookie cutter on sheet. Lift up cookie cutter and repeat with remaining meringue, forming six hearts on each sheet. Bake one hour or until meringues are crisp and dry. Cool for ten minutes and peel meringues off foil. Can be made a day ahead and stored in airtight container at room temperature. Top with vanilla ice cream and strawberries. If desired, drizzle meringues with chocolate sauce.

## CHEESE STRAWS

2 sticks margarine

2½ cups grated sharp cheddar cheese

2 cups flour

2 cups Rice Crispies® cereal

Walnuts or pecan halves

Mix margarine and cheese. Add flour. Mix well. Stir in Rice Crispies. Roll in walnut-sized balls and mash down with fork into cookie shape. Top with pecan or walnut half. Bake at 375° for 20 minutes or until light brown.

No *finer* hat can be found
Than one with *roses* all around.

SUSAN WALES

# Herb Luncheon

This is a lovely birthday luncheon for an honoree who loves to cook or a unique shower for a bride. Each guest brings a pot of herbs and a recipe that features the herb. The potted herbs are given to the guest-of-honor to start her own herb garden. The hostess provides a recipe keepsake box, file, or book for the collection of recipes.

## Invitations

Attach a sprig of rosemary to the invitations.

Vickie Strickland and Annie Suliman invite you to a
### BIRTHDAY LUNCHEON
Honoring Lynn Swindell
Bring a pot of herbs with a recipe
Date, Time, Place
RSVP: Telephone Number    Dress: Party Dress

## Menu

Basil Tomatoes with Grated Cheese
Rosemary Chicken with Parsley Rice
Mint Tea
Garlic Bread
Ginger Pears with Vanilla Ice Cream

## BASIL TOMATOES WITH GRATED CHEESE

*Serves 8*

4 medium tomatoes
2 tablespoons crushed basil
Olive oil

$^1/_2$ cup grated Parmesan cheese
Salt and pepper to taste

Wash tomatoes and slice in half. Do not peel. Salt and pepper tomatoes and drizzle with olive oil. Top with crushed basil and then Parmesan cheese. Broil for 10 minutes or until tomatoes are soft.

# GINGER PEARS WITH VANILLA ICE CREAM

*Serves 6*

Juice of 1 lemon
2 cups sugar
4 cups water

1 tablespoon ground ginger
6 firm, ripe pears
Sprigs of mint

Bring lemon juice, 1 cup sugar (set aside the other cup of sugar), water, and ginger to a boil, stirring until sugar dissolves. Cut pears in half and core. Place pears in sugar water. Cook until tender. Remove from heat. Store pears in sugar water in refrigerator until serving. Prior to serving, pour remaining sugar on waxed paper, remove pears from liquid, and coat with sugar. Place pears under broiler until golden brown. Serve with vanilla ice cream. Garnish with mint.

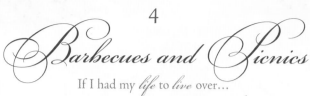

# 4
## Barbecues and Picnics

*If I had my life to live over…*
I would eat more *ice cream* and fewer *beans*.

BROTHER JEREMIAH

When daffodils peek their heads through the ground and pretty weather comes 'round, outdoor entertaining is just around the corner! Take your guests outdoors for a change of scenery. Burgers on the grill and seating guests on the patio is a perfect remedy for spring fever or a hot summer night. Never mind if smoke gets in your eyes or the ants vie for an invitation to your picnic, the setting will add a special ambiance to your affair.

## THINGS YOU NEED TO KNOW ABOUT COOKING OUTDOORS

+ Make sure your grill is clean and that you have all the proper utensils: a long-handled fork, tongs, spatula, and an oven mitt.

+ Lightly oil the grill's rack before cooking.

+ It takes about 45 minutes for coals to get hot. To test the coals, place your hand approximately six inches above the cooking surface. If you can leave your hand there for three to four seconds, the heat is medium (fish and chicken), and for only two seconds, the heat is high (beef and pork).

+ Pre-cook ribs and extra thick cuts of meat before grilling.

+ Brush barbecue sauce on only during the last several minutes of grilling to prevent it from dripping on the flames and burning your meat.

+ Never leave the grill unattended and keep a spray bottle of water beside the grill to control flames. Douse your fire when you leave.

# Tailgate Picnic

*Poultry* is for the *cook*
what canvas is *for* the painter.
BRILLAT-SAVARIN

Taking a meal to a sporting event has become a popular custom that allows you and your guests to arrive at the game, horse show, car race, or outdoor event well before the traffic. Relax in the parking lot with your open trunk serving as your buffet table or spread out the meal under a shady tree. Tailgate parties have become quite elaborate, and with the popular sport utility vehicles there is more space and convenience. Some hosts entertain in their recreational vehicles. The following tailgate party was designed for a college football game on a crisp fall afternoon.

## Invitations

For your invitations, design a football pennant in your school's colors or write on stationery the color of the school's colors.

Give me a "T"
What does it spell?
A Tailgate Picnic
Kick-off Picnic Time - Date and time
Place
Your hosts and cheerleaders...Joe and Denise Huey
RSVP: Telephone Number  Dress: Letter Sweater or School Colors

## Decorations and Flowers

Attach a team pennant on each corner of your vehicle. Bring along a bunch of colorful balloons to tie to the car. Decorate with crepe paper and have plenty of colored napkins on hand. Folding chairs and table are a must. For your centerpiece, fill a football helmet with large mums and

41

autumn leaves mingled with a team pennant, pompoms, and streamers atop a tablecloth in the team's colors.

## Name Tags

Cut football-shaped name tags out of brown paper bags.

## Music

Play a tape of your school's fight song, other marches, and football songs. Also, take along a radio to hear the pre-game show.

## ❧ Menu ❧

Guacamole Dip with Corn Chips and Veggies

Hearty Chili Served in Hollowed-Out Round Loaves

of Bread

Mexican Corn Muffins

Romaine Salad with Oranges and Avocados

Football-Shaped Chocolate Cake

## ROMAINE SALAD WITH ORANGES AND AVOCADOS

*Serves 4-6*

4 mandarin oranges peeled and segmented or 1 11-ounce can mandarin sections, drained

1 firm, ripe avocado, peeled and sliced

1 head of romaine lettuce torn into bite-size pieces

1 small purple onion, sliced

$1/2$ cup toasted slivered almonds
Salt and pepper to taste
Italian vinaigrette or balsamic vinegar dressing

Toss ingredients with dressing in a large salad bowl just prior to serving.

# MEXICAN CORN MUFFINS

1 1/2 cups self-rising corn meal

1/4 cup flour

1/2 teaspoon baking powder

2 eggs

3/4 cup buttermilk or regular milk

1 8 3/4-ounce can cream corn

1 cup grated cheese

3 jalepeno peppers (remove seeds)

1 medium onion, chopped

1/2 bell pepper, diced

1/3 cup cooking oil

Mix all ingredients except cheese. Pour half of mixture into a greased iron skillet. Cover with grated cheese and pour remaining mixture over that. Cook at 400° for 30 minutes.

# CHILI

*Serves 8*

3 pounds ground beef or 2 pounds ground beef and 1 pound of ground pork

1/2 cup each red and green pepper, chopped

1 cup onions, chopped

1 garlic clove, chopped

2 16-ounce cans tomatoes, crushed

2 11.6-ounce cans V8® Juice or Picante V8® Juice

2 16-ounce cans kidney beans, drained

2 to 4 tablespoons chili powder (to taste)

1 to 2 tablespoons dried red pepper flakes (optional)

1 tablespoon sugar

1 to 2 teaspoons each salt and pepper

1 bay leaf (optional)

Onions and/or grated cheese to garnish

Brown ground beef and pork in large skillet. Remove meat from skillet and sauté peppers and onions in drippings until golden brown and combine with meat in a large Dutch oven. Add remaining ingredients, cover, and simmer for 1 to 2 hours until thickened. Remove bay leaf and garnish with chopped onions and grated cheese. Serve with bread or tortilla chips. Can be made a day ahead and reheated.

# Watermelon Social

When *one* has tasted watermelon
He knows what the *angels* eat.

MARK TWAIN

A watermelon social offers an opportunity to gather a large crowd together from two o'clock to five o'clock in the afternoon. It's an easy but fun event that takes little time, money, and effort. There's nothing that tastes as good on a hot summer day as a ripe, ice-cold watermelon! Add a freezer of ice cream and favorite desserts to please your company. Arrange to play old-fashioned games on the lawn including croquet, badminton, volleyball, horseshoes, or Frisbee. Swimming is great if you have a lake or pool.

## Invitations

What else but a watermelon? Use red and green construction paper to design a slice of watermelon or write the invitation on bright red or green paper using a pen of the opposite color. Your guests' mouths will water the moment they receive these clever invitations!

Watermelons are ripe on the vine
Sample a bite of Summertime
Come one and come all...young and old!
### For an Afternoon Social
at the Williams' swimming hole
Fun, Food, and Frolic
Date, Time - 2:00 - 4:00 P.M.
RSVP: Telephone Number   Dress: Play Clothes and a Swimsuit

## *Decorations, Flowers, and Name Tags*

Set up long tables and cover with newspaper. For the centerpiece, scoop out a watermelon and fill it with wildflowers. When ready to serve, place watermelons on tables with knives, forks, spoons, and red and green napkins. Make watermelon-shaped name tags.

### *Menu*

Large Tubs of Lemonade, Soft Drinks, and Water
Watermelons
Assorted Chips and Dip
Homemade Pound Cakes
Old-Fashioned Pecan, Apple, and Peach Pies
Homemade Ice Cream Served in Sugar Cones

### EASY PECAN PIE

*Serves 6-8*

| | |
|---|---|
| 1 cup dark corn syrup | 1 teaspoon vanilla extract |
| 1/2 cup melted butter | 1/4 teaspoon salt |
| 1 cup sugar | 1 9-inch unbaked pie shell |
| 4 eggs, beaten | 2 cups pecans |

Combine sugar, butter, and corn syrup over low heat, stirring constantly until mixture thickens. Cool. Add eggs, salt, vanilla, and pecans. Mix well. Pour into an unbaked pie shell and bake 45 minutes at 350°.

# Let's Go to the Races Barbecue

Racing fans are springing up everywhere! Gather the crowd for a mouth-watering barbecue at the speedway or at your home to celebrate the Indy 500 or any car race.

## Invitations

Write your invitations on white stationery with a black-and-white checkerboard border or use white paper and a black marker!

> ### Let's Go to the Races with Kimberly and Keith Strickland
> Date
> Starting Time
> Time
> Pre-Race Barbecue with all the trimmings
> Place
> RSVP: Telephone Number   Dress: Casual

## Decorations, Flowers, and Name Tags

Hang a hubcap outlined with flowers on your front door for a special welcome wreath. Cover your serving table with a black-and-white-checked table cloth. Use black-and-white checkered flags in your centerpiece with flowers. Serve your barbecue in silver paper plates to resemble hubcaps or you can place the plates inside a hubcap for a no-spill serving tray! If you are outdoors, borrow old tires from a gas station or the tire dealership to use for seating. Use spark plugs for corn holders. Make checkered flag name tags.

## Music

Country music is a real hit with most racing fans. Play it softly in the background for a festive mood.

*Menu*

Barbecued Ribs and Chicken
Corn-on-the-Cob
Baked Beans, Potato Salad, and Cole Slaw
Banana Split Cake
Gallons of Iced Tea

## BANANA SPLIT CAKE

*Serves 12*

2 cups graham cracker crumbs
3 sticks margarine
5 bananas
2 cups powdered sugar

1 #2 can crushed pineapple
1 9-ounce carton Cool Whip®
1/2 cup nuts
1 small jar maraschino cherries

Mix 1 stick margarine with graham cracker crumbs. Pat into a 13 x 9 x 2 pan. Beat the remaining margarine and the powdered sugar with an electric mixer for 15 minutes. Spread over crust. Place sliced bananas on top. Spread can of pineapple over bananas. Cover with Cool Whip®, sprinkle with nuts, and decorate with cherries. Refrigerate overnight.

# The Scavenger Hunt

*Joy is a net of love*
by which you can catch *souls*.

MOTHER TERESA

This wild goose chase is loads of fun for teens and adults. A Scavenger Hunt is a party where the hosts provide a list of unusual items or items from nature that the guests have to go out and find and bring back to the party within a specified time limit to compete with the others for prizes or gag gifts! This party is conducive to a large group—a class, a church group, the gang at the office, or a team. The more the merrier!

As soon as your guests arrive, have them draw a number from a large fish bowl and go to the area marked by a balloon with their number to meet their team. Your guests will be divided into teams of 5 guests and each team will select their captain and a name for their team. Before they are sent on their way, a picnic-style dinner is served.

After dinner, the teams reconvene and the hosts hand out the lists of items to find. The guests are allowed to ask questions and then the hosts blow the whistle for the guests to leave. The team that brings back the most items on the list wins. After the prizes are awarded, dessert is served. Happy hunting!

## *Invitations*

These invitations are written on a treasure map that leads your guests through a maze of familiar and not-so-familiar locations to your home.

Seek and ye shall dine and find
### Scavenger Hunt
Gather at Betsy and Dick Hegg's
Date, Time
RSVP: Telephone Number      Dress: Casual

Be creative in assembling your list. It's amazing how the guests can figure out how to find the items without purchasing them.

### SAMPLE LIST FOR SCAVENGER HUNT

1. G. I. Joe doll
2. 60s Beatles album
3. A rotary telephone
4. A used ticket to a baseball game
5. Deer antler
6. Rhinestone sunglasses
7. Bus token
8. Baby's pacifier
9. Can of red paint
10. Seashell
11. A policeman's badge
12. A hamster

## *Decorations, Flowers, and Name Tags*

Balloons are great for this party. For the centerpiece use feathers and pine cones mixed with flowers. Everyone will need a name tag! Have each group decide upon a name for their team and make their own name tags. For example: Elvis' Elves. Be creative!

## Menu

*Hot Dog Bar with All the Trimmings*
*Condiment Bar: Chili, Relish, Onions, Sauerkraut,*
*Ketchup, Mustard*
*Refrigerator Cole Slaw*
*Potato Chips*
*Fruit and Vegetable Platters with Dips*
*Ice Cream Sundae Bar*
*Variety of Sauces, Nuts, Whipped Cream, Fruit Toppings,*
*Candy Toppings, and Sprinkles*

## REFRIGERATOR COLE SLAW

1 medium head cabbage, chopped
 fine or a two-pound package
 of pre-chopped lettuce
2 medium onions
1 small bell pepper
3 medium apples, chopped
1 teaspoon celery seed

1 teaspoon dried mustard
1 cup sugar
1 cup vinegar
$^3/4$ cup oil
1 tablespoon salt
2 teaspoons sugar

Chop cabbage and slice pepper and onions into thin rings. In a bowl layer cabbage, onions, pepper rings, and apples, alternating until full. Pour 1 cup of sugar on top. Bring to a boil vinegar, oil, sugar, mustard, celery seed, and salt. Pour over the cabbage mixture. Let cool, cover tightly, and refrigerate. Let stand in refrigerator for three days.

# Country Western Party

It's time to pull out your cowboy hats and boots and rustle up some grub for your friends and neighbors at this festive outdoor party. Turn your backyard into a corral. Spread hay or straw all over the party area. Bring in bales of hay for seating. You can purchase these or sometimes borrow them from the local nursery. Crank up the cowboy music and let the fun begin!

## Invitations

Make up Wanted Posters with a photograph of the host and hostess for fun. You can omit the photograph.

> # Wanted:
> ## The Whole Gang
> ### Reward: Barbecue and Line Dancing
> Date, Time
> Susan and Tom Lovell's Corral
> RSVP: Telephone Number    Dress: Western

## Decorations and Flowers

Cover the table in denim or red gingham and use a cowboy boot filled with flowers for the centerpiece. Serve snacks in children's cowboy hats. Use aluminum pie pans for serving pieces and offer your guests drinks in Mason jars. Use colorful bandannas tied with rope for napkins. Hang lanterns to light up the backyard. Hang wanted posters and place pots of cactus around for decorations. Light a campfire if not prohibited.

## Place Cards and Name Tags

Make name tags to resemble a sheriff's badge. If there is individual seating, mark each place with gold nuggets in a pouch. You can buy gold nugget bubble gum in a pouch and personalize it with a gold marker or place small pebbles sprayed gold and tied in a piece of cloth with raffia.

## *Music*

Have plenty of tapes with western music such as "Home on the Range," "Happy Trails to You," "Red River Valley," or "Buffalo Gals." You can also have your guests sit around the campfire and sing old western songs. For a real treat, hire an instructor or ask a friend to teach everyone line dancing or the Texas Two-Step. Swing your partner!

### *Menu*

Barbecued Beef or Steaks
Baked Beans
Coleslaw
Barbecue Bread
Texas Chocolate Cake

## TEXAS CHOCOLATE CAKE

| | |
|---|---|
| 1 cup water | 1 cup sour cream |
| 4 tablespoons cocoa | 2 cups unsifted flour |
| 2 cups sugar | 1 teaspoon soda |
| 1/2 teaspoon salt | 2 eggs, beaten |
| 2 sticks butter | 1 teaspoon vanilla |

Bring water, butter, and cocoa to a boil. Remove from heat and add rest of ingredients. Beat until smooth and well-blended. Pour into a greased and floured 12 x 18 cake pan or jelly roll pan. Bake at 375° for 25 minutes.

## ICING

| | |
|---|---|
| 1 stick butter | 4 tablespoons cocoa |
| 6 tablespoons milk | 1 cup chopped pecans |
| 1 pound confectioners' sugar | 1 teaspoon vanilla |

Bring to boil butter, cocoa, and milk. Remove from heat and add rest of ingredients. Spread icing on lukewarm cake.

# 5
## Dinner Parties

*If you accept a* dinner *invitation—you have the* moral
*obligation to be* amusing.

THE DUTCHESS OF WINDSOR

The dinner party is the most popular way of entertaining family and friends. To make party-planning simple, select a theme to carry throughout the party with the invitations, the decor, and the food.

A plan is not always necessary. If you are so inspired on a pretty evening, invite your friends over at the last minute for a potluck supper. These impromptu events can sometimes turn into the most memorable times of all!

Your party can range anywhere from casual to elegant. Don't hesitate to use paper plates or order pizza. When it comes to eating, we are blessed to live in an age where anything goes (there are no hard and fast rules). Sometimes it's fun just to celebrate life and being together. Yet, it is also very special when you bring out your best china, crystal, and silver to entertain your guests. Try both ways!

Dinner should be served approximately forty-five minutes after all your guests have arrived and been warmly welcomed. While they become acquainted with the other guests or catch up with old friends, serve light hors d'oeuvres. Plan on approximately five bites per person so your guests will still have an appetite when dinner is served.

Your personal style can transform your dinner into a memorable evening. Serve delicious food, dim the lights, light a fire and candles for a special evening, but most of all make your guests feel welcome.

After dinner, invite your guests into the living room, onto the terrace, or another area to serve coffee and dessert. Unless there is entertainment, it is proper for your guests to leave forty-five minutes after dessert is served.

# Titanic Dinner Party

Stage your own Titanic Party using a nautical theme and serve your favorite seafood dishes. Spread sand in your backyard and kick off your shoes for an evening of ocean fun.

## Invitations

For your invitations, use red, white, and blue construction paper to make a life preserver. Use a red marker to write your invitations. For simpler invitations, write on red, white, or blue construction paper.

> ### For a Whale of a Good Time
> Float on over to the Wales'
> Titanic Dinner Party
> Date and Time
> Place
> RSVP: Phone number    Dress: Nautical

## Decorations and Flowers

Carry the red, white, and blue nautical theme throughout your house. Overlay your dining room tablecloth with fishnets and seashells. For the centerpiece, fill a box covered in flowers or metallic paper or a treasure chest with faux pearls, jewels, and gold coins. Float red, white, and blue candles or goldfish in fish bowls that you can give as prizes when the evening ends. Create an iceberg out of crushed ice filled with shrimp in the center for hors d'oeuvres. Serve food in shells, shell-shaped casserole dishes, pineapple boats, or coconut shells.

## Place Cards and Name Tags

Personalized seashells make great place cards. If you serve buffet, you can give your guests the shells as party favors. Attach gold seals to resemble gold coins to name tags.

## Music

Play the soundtrack from the movie *Titanic* alternating with tapes of crashing waves and water to add a special ambiance to your party.

## *Menu*

Shrimp with Cocktail Sauce
Steaming Clam Chowder or Crab Bisque
Strawberry Spinach or Romaine Salad
Flounder Casserole
Tomatoes Stuffed with Carrots and Peas
Croissants
Madeleines

## STRAWBERRY SPINACH OR ROMAINE SALAD

*Serves 4*

3 quarts fresh spinach or romaine lettuce

4 cups sliced fresh strawberries

1 medium purple onion, sliced

$1/2$ cup crumbled feta cheese

$1/2$ cup walnuts

Toss with Italian dressing.

## CRAB BISQUE

2 cups flaked crab meat

$1/2$ cup cooking sherry

1 $10^1/2$-ounce can cream of tomato soup

1 $10^1/2$-ounce can green pea soup

1 cup half and half

$1/2$ teaspoon curry powder

1 teaspoon paprika

Place crab meat in bowl, add sherry, and toss lightly. Pour all other ingredients into a saucepan over low heat. Add crab meat and heat. Garnish with parsley and serve hot.

# FLOUNDER CASSEROLE

*Serves 6*

1½ pounds of flounder filets, cut up

1 10¾ ounce-can cream of shrimp soup, undiluted

1 tablespoon Worcestershire sauce

1 tablespoon onion juice

1 teaspoon garlic juice

1 tablespoon lemon rind

Salt and pepper

24 Ritz® crackers

Salt and pepper flounder filets and place in a greased 9 x 13 casserole dish. Mix soup, Worcestershire sauce, onion, and garlic juice and pour over flounder. Cook at 350° for 20-25 minutes. Crush Ritz® crackers into crumbs and mix with melted butter. Top casserole with cracker crumbs and cook for an additional ten minutes. Garnish with parsley and lemon slices.

# MADELEINES

*14 cakes*

These tea cakes are baked in scalloped madeleine shells or you can use muffin tins.

¾ cup butter, melted

2 eggs

1 cup sugar

1 cup sifted cake flour

1 teaspoon vanilla

In a double boiler heat eggs and sugar, stirring constantly, until warm. Remove from heat and beat until light and creamy. Cool and gradually add flour. Pour in melted butter and vanilla. Pour mixture into madeleine shells and bake at 350° for about 8 minutes until golden brown. If muffin tin is used, double cooking time. Invert and cool on a rack, shell side up.

# Harvest Soup Supper

*I feel that a recipe is only a theme,*
*which an intelligent cook*
*can play each time with a variation.*

MADAME BENOIT

Fall is in the air! As the season arrives, nature provides an abundance of food, plants, and flowers in a wide spectrum of colors, scents, and textures. Our thoughts turn to autumn leaves, apples, chilly evenings with crackling fires, and hearty soups. It's also back-to-school time, football games, and bonfires. The busy summer has come to an end, and it's time to round up our friends and neighbors for a Harvest Party. Transform your home into a harvest farm to celebrate the season!

## Invitations

Make your invitations in fall shapes such as sunflowers, pumpkins, or apples or decorate colorful pieces of paper with vegetable stickers.

> ## Shine On Harvest Moon···
> Fall is in the Air!
> Come for a Souper Supper
> at Ann and Linton Dangar's Farm
> Date, Time
> RSVP: Telephone Number     Dress: Jeans

## Decorations, Flowers, and Name Tags

Nature's bounty will provide the setting. Bring the scarecrow in from the garden to greet the guests. You can buy this harvest doll stuffed with straw and place him in a rocking chair near the entrance or hang him on a wall or on the lamppost among the cornstalks. Write each guest's name on an autumn leaf with a gold marker and pin it on your harvest greeter, then have each guest find his or her name tag. Make sure the leaves you choose are not brittle or dry.

Adorn your door with a wreath of sunflowers, colorful corn, gourds, and vegetables. Stack corn stalks on each side of the door with a group of pumpkins. Flank the door with hay bales and two baskets filled will fall apples—golden, green, and red. When the guests depart, supply them with small brown bags to pick apples to take home with them.

Serve a variety of soups in a pumpkin patch! Cover your serving counter or table with green moss and prop corn stalks at each end. Twine pumpkin or morning glory vines and blooms along the edge. Scoop out pumpkins and fill them with steaming soups. To identify each soup, label the pumpkins and surround them with some of their ingredients, such as dried corn for corn chowder and tomatoes for tomato soup. Make soup ladles out of scooped-out dried gourds. Serve apple cider out of a big tin tub.

A bonfire is always great if you live in an area where they are permitted. Otherwise, start a fire in the fireplace. Outside, have a variety of games set up for your guests: horseshoes, apple bobbing, a three-legged race. Play a game of Pin-the-Heart-on-the-Scarecrow.

## *Music*

This is a festive indoor and outdoor occasion. Blue grass music is always a hit at a Harvest Party!

## *Menu*

Tossed Green Salad
Crusty French Bread, Corn Muffins
New England Clam Chowder
Corn Chowder
Vegetable-Sausage Soup
Hot Apple Cider
Brownies, Congo Bars, and Lemon Squares

# CORN CHOWDER WITH CHICKEN

*8 cups*

$^1/_2$ stick butter

1 cup chopped onions

$^1/_2$ cup chopped green pepper

Salt and pepper to taste

$^1/_2$ teaspoon paprika

$^1/_2$ cup chopped pimentos

2 cups canned or fresh corn

2 cups potatoes, cubed

2 cups cooked chicken, cubed

3 cups boiling water

2 tablespoons butter

3 tablespoons flour

2 cups milk or half and half

Melt ½ stick of butter, then add onions and green pepper and sauté until softened. Add salt, pepper, pimentos, corn, potatoes, chicken, and water. Cook for 15 minutes. In another pan, melt 2 tablespoons butter, mix in flour until smooth; add milk gradually until thickened. Pour into corn mixture. Cook until slightly thickened. Serve hot.

# NEW ENGLAND CLAM CHOWDER

*8 cups*

4 cans (6$^3/_4$-ounces) minced clams

1 medium onion, diced

Salt and pepper to taste

3 medium potatoes

6 tablespoons butter

3 cups milk

Drain clams and reserve juice. Peel potatoes and cut up. Melt 2 tablespoons butter over medium heat, add onion, and sauté until tender. Add clam juice and potatoes and bring to a boil. Reduce heat and simmer until potatoes are tender. Add clams, remaining butter, milk, and salt and pepper until heated thoroughly.

# HOT MULLED APPLE CIDER

*Serves 32*

| | |
|---|---|
| 1 gallon apple cider | 4 tablespoons whole cloves |
| 1 6-ounce can frozen lemonade, undiluted | 1 medium orange, sliced |
| 4 cinnamon sticks | 2 medium apples, sliced |

Mix together and heat cider, lemonade, cinnamon sticks, and 2 tablespoons cloves. Remove spices and place in a punch bowl. Float apple and oranges slices studded with remaining cloves on top. Serve hot.

## Mystery Dinner

Everyone loves a good mystery! People enjoy the excitement of the unknown. Make plans for this adventuresome evening at home. We recommend purchasing a Murder Mystery Game. There are several available for such an evening or, if you are a mystery buff, you can concoct your own mystery. Assign each one of your guests a part to play. Have everyone design their own mask to wear to the party and give a prize for the most original mask, the funniest mask, the most beautiful mask, and the ugliest mask.

### Invitations

Cut your invitations into pieces that your guests will have to fit together! Each piece of the puzzle will have a different item of information on it. For example, the invitation below would be cut into five pieces.

### It's a Mystery

Where? The Tuckers' Home
When? Date and Time
What? Mystery Dinner Evening
RSVP: Telephone Number   Dress: Design a Mask

## Decorations, Place Cards, and Name Tags

Make black construction paper footprints leading up to the front door. Staple names onto black masks as place cards for each guest. For the centerpiece, decorate with handcuffs, a rope, and a toy knife and gun. Each guest will wear a name tag that identifies both their character and their own name.

## Music

Real spooky music will add to the atmosphere of the party!

## Menu

This is the perfect evening to set up a pasta bar with a variety of sauces. Your guests can choose one of the sauces below or try all three!

### Pasta Bar

*Italian Bean Salad*
*Three Kinds of Pasta (Half Pound per Person):*
*Fettucine, Spaghetti, Angel Hair*
*Sauces: Marinara, Alfredo, Italian Meat Sauce*
*Fresh Grated Romano and Parmesan Cheese*
*Garlic Bread; Lemon Meringue Pie*

## ITALIAN BEAN SALAD

*Serves 8*

| | |
|---|---|
| 1 pound green beans, cooked | 1 tablespoon sugar |
| $1/2$ pound yellow wax beans | 3 tablespoons vinegar |
| 1 19-ounce can chick peas | $1/4$ cup olive oil |
| 1 $15^1/4$-ounce can kidney beans | 1 tablespoon oregano |
| $1^1/2$ cups chopped celery | 1 teaspoon salt |
| 1 medium red onion, chopped | $1/2$ teaspoon pepper |

Combine beans, chick peas, celery, and onion in a large bowl. Mix ingredients for dressing and toss with beans.

# Potluck Supper Club

Nothing is *particularly* hard
if you *divide* it into *small* jobs.

HENRY FORD

Gather three to four couples to take turns hosting a potluck supper once a month. The hosts will select the party theme and assign each couple a dish to bring. Celebrate with a special holiday theme or food from another country. This is an excellent way to perfect your cooking. The following potluck party was designed around a Mexican theme.

## Invitations

Design a sombrero on colorful paper of red, green, orange, or yellow or write invitations on colorful paper with a different color pen.

### Harriot and Bob Hall

Have a dinner party under their sombrero!
Join us South of the Border at 345 Davis Drive
Please bring a Mexican dessert for eight
Time, Date, Place
RSVP: Phone Number  Dress: Bright Colors

## Decorations and Flowers

Line your sidewalk with luminarias. Also, place them in your backyard around a pool, fountain, or edge of the lawn. Hang a chili pepper wreath on your front door and a colorful piñata on the porch! Cover your table with a brightly colored cloth and accent with napkins of red, yellow, orange, or green. Use a Mexican serape or a colorful blanket or cloth as a table runner or center on the table.

A large arrangement of sunflowers, colorful corn, and branches of peppers makes a great centerpiece. Scoop out colorful red, green, and yellow peppers to hold votive candles to place around the table and the rooms. Serve your dinner in clay saucers.

## *Music*

Who doesn't enjoy mariachi music? Play a selection of Mexican music in the background.

## *Menu*

Taco Dip
Entree: Fajita Bar
Corn and Flour Tortillas
Grilled Chicken and Steak
Grated Cheese, Shredded Lettuce, Sour Cream,
Green Onions, Cilantro,
Guacamole, Rice, and Salsa Served in Brightly Colored
Pottery Bowls
Vegetable: Roasted Corn

## TACO DIP

| | |
|---|---|
| 1 can refried beans or black beans | 1 cup chopped green onions |
| 3 cups guacamole dip | $^3/_4$ cup sharp cheddar cheese |
| $^1/_2$ cup chopped tomatoes | $^1/_2$ cup mild taco sauce |
| $^1/_3$ cup chopped green pepper | $^1/_2$ cup ranch dressing |

Spread beans in a 10" glass pie plate. Layer tomatoes, green peppers, and onions and top with cheese. Drizzle with taco sauce and ranch dressing. Serve with corn chips.

# Oscar Night Party

The basic thing which contributes to *charm*
is the ability to *forget* oneself and be
*engrossed* in other people.

ELEANOR ROOSEVELT

Invite your movie buff friends over for an evening at the Oscars. Borrow televisions to set up in each room if you invite a large crowd. Dress either to the nines or casually and greet your guests at the door with a camera for their souvenir photo. Enjoy a buffet of delicious food or Chinese take-out. This is also a great potluck party. Be creative in selecting your theme. Name your food items for movies. Make ballots for your guests and give gag prizes to winners. Be prepared for more than one winner.

## Invitations

Write your invitations on star-bordered paper or star cut-outs.

### The Stars Are Coming Out
ON OSCAR NIGHT
DATE AND TIME
JOIN US AT THE WATKINS' HOUSE
BUFFET
RSVP: Telephone Number    DRESS: Formal or Casual

## Decorations, Flowers, and Name Tags

Scatter silver confetti everywhere, and hang silver stars and mylar balloons from the ceiling. Ask your local video rental store for outdated movie posters. For the centerpiece, use flowers with silver sparkles. Use silver stars for name tags.

## Music

Play movie themes before the show begins.

## ❧ Menu ❧

*The Godfather Lasagna*

*When Harry Met Sally Tossed Green Salad*

*As Good As It Gets Three Bean Salad*

*Casablanca Garlic Bread*

*Forrest Gump Chocolate Pie*

## FORREST GUMP CHOCOLATE PIE

$1^1/_2$ cups plain flour
$1^1/_2$ sticks margarine
 2 cups chopped pecans
 3 cups milk

8 ounces cream cheese, softened
1 9-ounce container Cool Whip®
2 3-ounce packages instant chocolate pudding
2 cups sliced strawberries or bananas
1 cup confectioners' sugar

Mix together flour, butter, and 1½ cups pecans. Press into a 9 x 13 glass dish and bake at 350° for 30 minutes. Mix confectioners' sugar, cream cheese, and half of the Cool Whip®. Put this mixture in the cooled crust. Cover with strawberries or bananas. Mix chocolate pudding with 3 cups of milk and pour on top of cream cheese mixture. Then top with remaining Cool Whip and sprinkle with nuts. Chill, cut into squares, and serve.

# 6
## Unique Parties

*Happiness is a perfume that you cannot pour on others without getting a few drops on yourself.*

GEORGE BERNARD SHAW

Growing up in small towns, especially small southern towns, we learn at a very early age that hospitality is not just about parties, teas, and balls. True hospitality is meeting the needs of others. It is the art of bringing people together for fun and fellowship and sharing both the good and bad times alike.

As teenagers, we were constantly looking for any excuse to throw a party...anything to get our friends together! We grew up in the era of spend-the-night parties. There were never any boys allowed, well, only in our conversation. We brought along our favorite records (and for those of you who don't know...records are the equivalent to today's compact discs), gigantic pink hair rollers, hot pink nail polish, and what sleep-over over would be complete without your latest baby doll pajamas? We enjoyed a night of dancing and munching coupled with intense and cutting-edge beauty make-overs. The following day, we would go home and go straight to bed where we would make up for lost shut-eye.

It is our belief that you are never too old to enjoy the pleasures of a spend-the-night party. In keeping with this belief, we have designed the ultimate spa party complete with healthy food ideas (we promise not to tell if you substitute good old junk food instead...chips, dips, chocolate, and pizza)!

Another one of our unique party suggestions is a get-well party. This is an ideal way to bring a little sunshine and joyful laughter to a friend on the mend. If your friend feels up to it and is ready for a change, then give her a make-over complete with a facial, manicure, and new hairdo. There's nothing like looking good to make you feel good!

Our last unique party idea is one that will bring all of your friends together easily and effortlessly—a movie party! Be creative. You might want to plan your movie party around a particular theme or a holiday.

With all of these parties, the key to remember is to be creative and happy. These are great ways to bring people together and to really laugh with each other. Hospitality is about the giving and receiving of joy with your friends. Just remember to reserve a leisurely Saturday morning for recuperation!

## Slumber Spa Party

Get the girls together for a night of pampering and beauty. The guest of honor, the birthday girl, gets *the works* and all the guests join in the fun...but no guys allowed! Guests can bring the honoree bath oils, lotions, and other beauty products as gifts.

### Invitations

Trace a small hand mirror and cut it out of pink construction paper for cute invitations. Write the invitations on the mirror with a colored pen. For a simpler invitation, use hot pink stationery and a contrasting pen.

> ### Mirror, Mirror in My Hand
> Who's the fairest in the land?
> For the answer...
> Come celebrate Ruth's Birthday
> at Ivey and Megan's Slumber Spa
> Date, Time, Place
> RSVP: Telephone Number   Dress: Pajamas

### Decorations and Flowers

Fill an antique pitcher with flowers used in beauty products—such as roses and lavender—to create a beautiful centerpiece for your slumber party. Place a bunch of birthday balloons outside on the lamppost or the mailbox. Mark each designated beauty area with a birthday balloon. Place aromatic candles throughout.

73

## Details

Set up the spa complete with nail polish, manicure tools, cotton balls, oils, and lotions, and prepare an area for facials and make-up. These individual facial packs can be purchased inexpensively at the local drugstore. A few *au naturale* potions can be mixed in the kitchen including an egg-and-corn-meal mask, an avocado mask, and sliced ice-cold cucumbers for the eyes. Fill baskets with an abundance of washcloths and towels and place nearby. Rollers, curling irons, conditioners, and other hair products should be readily available. Have hair styling magazines for the guests to peruse.

## Music

Play Goldie Oldies from all the decades—fifties, sixties, seventies, and eighties! And an exercise video with music is also fun.

## Menu

*Fruit Smoothies*

*Stir Fry Tofu and Broccoli with Brown Rice*

*Salad*

*Birthday Cake—You've Gotta Have Cake!*

## FRUIT SMOOTHIE

### Combine the following in a blender:

1½ chilled unsweetened pineapple
juice

1 ripe banana

1 cup sliced strawberries

2 teaspoons honey
Juice of 1 lime

½ cup finely crushed ice

# Get-Well/Cheer-Up Party

A smiling face is half the meal.

LATVIAN PROVERB

It's customary to lend a helping hand to friends with a new baby or who have had an accident, surgery, or chemotherapy. We've taken the custom a step further and staged a get-well party for a friend. Another friend included a hat-making party for her friend undergoing chemotherapy, and others have taken their movable feast to a friend or relative in a nursing home.

The Cheer-Up Party is organized by a group of friends who will bring food, pretty paper napkins, paper plates, and flowers for a luncheon. Friends will do all the work and entertain in the shut-in's own home. The luncheon will be served at the table or, if the friend is bed-ridden, on trays in her room. You can double your recipe or bring extra casseroles for dinner or the freezer so your greetings can be extended to the rest of the family for the evening meal. Set the table before you go!

## Menu

*Chicken Soup*
*Popovers*
*Egg Custard with Fruit*

## POPOVERS

| | |
|---|---|
| 1 cup milk | 1/4 teaspoon salt |
| 1 tablespoon melted butter | 2 eggs |
| 1 cup sifted all-purpose flour | |

Preheat oven to 450°. Mix together milk, butter, flour, and salt. Beat eggs one at a time. Add to batter. Fill buttered deep muffin pans three-fourths full. Bake for 15 minutes and then lower the heat to 350° and bake 20 minutes longer. Remove popovers and serve hot with preserves and butter.

# Housewarming Party

You have moved into a cute fixer-upper and it's time to invite your friends to your new home for a party to kick off your home improvement projects! This is a fun and creative party that will allow your friends to see your new home "before." One clever couple had a "before" party and the next year invited the gang back again for the "after" party!

## Invitations

There are lots of cute housewarming cards available. If you would like to make your own, simply draw a house.

### Housewarming Party
We're eating beans!
Bring an ingredient for stone soup!
Courtney and Michael Norton's
Address
Time, Date
RSVP: Telephone     Dress: Jeans

## Decorations, Flowers, and Name Tags

Because you are saving your money for house remodeling, it is only natural to base your party theme on pinching pennies. Cover the table with newspaper—the want ads and the real estate ads! For your centerpiece, fill an empty paint can with flowers and paintbrushes. Place paint and wallpaper swatches on the wall, fabric samples on the coffee table, and serve snacks in hard hats or paint cans.

## Menu

Stone Soup
Copper Pennies
Tossed Green Salad
Bread

## STONE SOUP

The hostess provides a big stew pot filled with water and beans and each guest brings a vegetable for the soup.

## COPPER PENNIES

5 cups peeled and sliced carrots
1 cup thinly sliced onion
1 small green pepper, finely sliced
1 10³/4-ounce can tomato soup
¹/2 cup salad oil

¹/2 cup sugar
1 teaspoon dried mustard
1 teaspoon Worcestershire sauce
1 teaspoon salt
1 teaspoon pepper

Cook carrots until crisp; not soft. Toss with onion and green pepper. Combine rest of ingredients and pour over carrots. Marinate in refrigerator overnight and serve chilled.

## Movie Party

The *secret* ingredient I add
to all my recipes is *love*.

SUSAN WALES

For a fun but easy party, plan a relaxed evening for a small group of friends to gather round the television after dinnertime for a movie and snacks.

### Invitations

Design your invitations in the format of a movie ticket or write your invitations on empty popcorn bags. Another fun idea is to hand-deliver an empty video case with the invitation tucked inside. You can purchase these cases at a nominal fee at your local video store if you don't have extra ones on hand.

You'll Find
## The Movie & The Popcorn
Kim Lewis' House
Date and Time
RSVP: Telephone Number  Dress: Casual

## *Decorations and Flowers*

Ask your local movie theater for outdated movie posters. Use these to decorate your own "movie theater." Make a flower arrangement in a bag of popcorn. If there is a theme to your movie such as airplanes, hang paper or balsa airplanes from the ceiling. Or if your movie is a romantic comedy, hang hearts from the ceiling. For *Sleepless in Seattle*, you could hang maps and travel scenes from the city. Quiet please...lights, camera, action!

## *Music*

Play the film's soundtrack plus a variety of other movie soundtracks. Be sure that the music stops when the show begins!

## *Menu*

Hot Buttered Popcorn
Raisinettes®
Goobers®
Junior Mints®
Milk Duds®
Twizzlers®
Sweet Tarts®
Cokes® on Ice

# 7
# Holiday Celebrations

Small *cheer* and great welcome
Makes a *merry* feast.

WILLIAM SHAKESPEARE

*H*olidays offer us a wonderful opportunity to gather family and friends together. You'll start off the New Year with a bang! Your love will then abound on Valentine's Day, you'll ignite fireworks with your Fourth of July Celebration, and at Christmas you will focus on Christ's birth, your family, and giving! There's no better time to celebrate and establish traditions than the holidays.

Just imagine Christmas, the most festive time of the year. Houses twinkle with bright lights and halls are decked with greenery and holly. Delicious pine scents mingle with the fragrant aroma of cookies, pies, cakes, and breads. Bells are ringing and Christmas carols are sung at church, at home, and on every street corner. There's no better time to be with our friends and families as we celebrate the season and the birth of our Savior.

The New Year reminds us that the old has passed away as we celebrate new beginnings! Many of us ring out the previous year and welcome in the New Year with parties, festivities, or just gathering with our loved ones to count our many blessings.

Love is in the air when February 14 comes around. We celebrate with romantic candlelight dinners for two, boxes of heart-shaped chocolates and roses. Whether you are preparing for an intimate rendezvous with the one you love or a gathering of friends and family, Valentine's Day is a great occasion for fun and romantic entertaining.

We picnic on Memorial Day, the Fourth of July, and Labor Day as we celebrate and remember the special events and people of our nation. Thoughts of the great American picnic with its hamburgers, hot dogs, potato salad, watermelon, and much more makes our mouths water. In July, the day finally comes to a spectacular close as we watch the fireworks light up the summer sky with magnificent colors, soaring sounds, and brilliant radiance.

Yes, there's no time like the holidays to celebrate life and to be with the people you hold most dear!

## New Year's Eve Progressive Dinner

Several couples in surrounding neighborhoods can get together to host a group of friends for a Progressive Dinner Party and congregate the next morning for a New Year's Day Brunch. The guests can stay off the highways and walk or drive a short distance to each house where a dinner course is served. This party is a great way for young people to get started entertaining and for older busier couples to lighten their entertaining load.

### Invitations

List the courses, names of hosts, and addresses on individual keys cut from silver paper and attach to silver cord key rings. The guests must bring their keys to be admitted to the party. Ideally, the guests should arrive at the next-to-last house, Key #5, just before midnight but still with ample time to prepare to welcome in the New Year.

Key #1
New Year's Eve Party
Ring out the old!
Date and Time of Party
Gather at the Golds' House
Hors d'oeuvres
Address

Key #2
Appetizer
Name and Address of Hosts

Key #3
Salad Course
Name and Address of Hosts

Key #4
Main Course
Name and Address of Hosts

Key #5
Welcome in the New Year
Dessert and Coffee
Name and Address of Hosts

Key #6
Happy New Year
New Year's Day Brunch
The Carters' and Address
RSVP: Telephone Number   Dress: Coat and Tie, Party Clothes

## Details

Guests will meet at the first house in the late afternoon for hors d'oeuvres. The hosts will pin a name tag (a paper noisemaker with streamers) on each guest. The first three homes will remain decorated for Christmas. This will remind the guests of *the old year* which is giving way to the New Year.

## Decorations and Flowers

As the guests enter the home for the candlelight main course, the New Year hour will be fast approaching, so the hosts will have their home decorated for the coming year. The dining room table is covered with a white tablecloth and centered with a silver-glitter top hat filled with roses and surrounded with sparkling tinsel and silver confetti atop a mirror encircled by candles.

The house where dessert and coffee is served is the setting for a festive celebration. Candles atop mirrors are placed throughout the entertaining area. Exquisite desserts line the dining room table. Another silver-glitter top hat, this time filled with flowers, silver helium balloons, silver sparklers, and surrounded by silver confetti, centers the table. Silver helium balloons with ribbon streamers and Happy New Year banners hang *en masse* from the ceiling of the dining room. The host passes silver trays of noisemakers, horns, whistles, and streamers for each guest. The moment midnight arrives, the guests will welcome in the New Year!

## Music

Taking a cue from the famous Casey Kasem, it's fun to play all the top hits of the passing year for this festive occasion. Also, classical music played softly in the background is very nice. If the couples can pool their resources, it's really special to hire a pianist or a harpist for the evening. Sometimes the other couples who are not hosting will pitch in and provide the music. At midnight, (what else?) "Auld Lang Syne" is played.

## Dinner Menu

*Hors d'oeuvres*
Crisp Vegetables Served in a Silver Top Hat
Confetti Dip
Hot Artichoke Dip with Assorted Crackers
Miniature Ham and Cheese Biscuits
Punch and Sparkling Grape Juice
Appetizer: Bisque Served in Hollow Acorn Squash Shells
Salad: Greens with Raspberry Vinaigrette
Main Course: Beef Tenderloin
Vegetables: Green Beans Almondine
Broiled Herbed Tomatoes
Potatoes Anna
Dessert: Chocolate Mousse, Eclairs

# CONFETTI DIP

1 package onion soup mix

1 pint sour cream

$^{1}/_{4}$ cup green pepper, diced

$^{1}/_{4}$ cup red pepper, diced

$^{1}/_{4}$ cup water chestnuts, diced

$^{1}/_{4}$ cup black olives, diced

Combine all ingredients and chill for one hour. Serve with crackers or chips.

# HOT ARTICHOKE DIP

1 5-ounce can water chestnuts, chopped

1 13$^{3}/_{4}$-ounce can artichokes, drained

1 cup mayonnaise

1 cup Parmesan cheese

Drain, quarter, and mash artichokes. Add mayonnaise, Parmesan cheese, and water chestnuts. Put mixture into an oven-proof dish and heat in oven at 350° for 30 minutes. Serve hot with crackers.

# SPINACH DIP

1 10-ounce package chopped spinach

1 cup mayonnaise

1 cup sour cream

1 5-ounce small can water chestnuts, chopped

1 small onion, chopped

1 $^{5}/_{8}$-ounce package Knorrs® Vegetable Soup Mix

1 tablespoon lemon juice

1 round loaf of bread or a large, red cabbage

Thaw spinach and drain. Do not cook. Mix mayonnaise and sour cream with vegetable soup mix. Combine with spinach, onion, and water chestnuts. Chill spinach mixture for one hour. Hollow out round loaf of bread or purple cabbage and fill with spinach mixture when ready to serve. Serve with bread, raw vegetables, or crackers.

# CHOCOLATE MOUSSE

*8 servings*

20 chocolate-covered mints

1 cup chocolate morsels

$^{1}/_{3}$ cup sugar

3 eggs

1$^{1}/_{2}$ cups milk

1 pint whipping cream

Blend morsels and mints on high in blender. Whip 1/2 pint cream and sugar and add to chocolate mix in blender. Scald 1/2 cup of milk over low heat and add eggs, stirring for 30 seconds. Pour into blender. Add additional milk and blend all ingredients together on high. Pour into individual custard dishes or in large bowl and refrigerate overnight. Before serving whip remaining cream. Garnish mousse with whipped cream.

## The Morning After Brunch

Serve *your* guests as if they're
visiting *royalty*.
ANN PLATZ

The next morning, the hosts of the New Year's Day Brunch will have their home decked out for the New Year. Guests will be greeted by a large Happy New Year banner at the door. Arriving guests will immediately congregate at the coffee bar. To set up, please refer to the coffee bar in Chapter 2 on page 16. The dining room table is laid out with a brunch fit for a king and queen, including the South's traditional greens and black-eyed peas! The hosts from the night before have loaned the new hosts the silver top hat. The silver mylar balloons will float for several days, so the arrangement still looks fresh. Televisions for ball games are turned on in the family room, and the living room is set aside for quiet conversation. The children are playing in the bedrooms. Everyone wears a name tag that is inscribed with *Happy New Year* and their name.

## Menu

Juice and Coffee Bar
Egg-and-Sausage Casserole
Garlic Grits and Biscuits
Honey Ham and Sausages
Asparagus with Hollandaise Sauce
Black-Eyed Peas and Turnip Greens
Coconut Sour Cream Layer Cake

# EGG-AND-SAUSAGE CASSEROLE

*Serves 12*

6 slices white bread

1 pound hot sausage

1 teaspoon dry mustard

5 eggs, beaten

2¼ cups milk

1½ cups sharp shredded cheese

1 teaspoon salt

dash of Tabasco®

Cook and crumble sausage, drain fat. Cut crusts off bread, then butter and cube. Place bread in a 9 x 13 casserole dish. Sprinkle with sausage. Top with cheese. Mix together eggs, mustard, milk, salt, and Tabasco®. Refrigerate overnight. Bake at 350° for 35-40 minutes.

# COCONUT SOUR CREAM LAYER CAKE

1 package butter flavored or yellow cake mix

2 cups sugar

1½ cups whipped topping

1 16-ounce carton sour cream

1 12-ounce package coconut

Prepare cake mix according to package directions, making two 8" layers. Combine sugar, sour cream, and coconut, blending well; chill. Reserve 1 cup coconut mixture for frosting; spread remainder between layers of cake. Combine reserved cup of coconut mixture with whipped topping; blend until smooth. Spread on top and sides of cake. Seal cake in airtight container. Refrigerate for three days before serving.

# *Singles' Valentine Party*

There's nothing like Valentine's Day to spark a little romance. This party is a fun mixer and buffet for singles. Couples and families can customize this same party with a different twist! This hearts-and-flowers celebration doesn't even have to be held on Valentine's Day! It's also a great event for an engagement, anniversary, or wedding party.

For a costume party, ask your guests to come as famous lovers such as Romeo and Juliet, Popeye and Olive Oyl, or Scarlett O'Hara and Rhett Butler.

## Invitations

Cut hearts out of red construction paper and paste them on white doilies. Write invitations with colored markers. Take another red heart and cut it in half. Write the name of a famous couple on each half. Include a half-heart with a woman's name in a woman's invitation and half-heart with a man's name in a man's invitation. When the guests arrive at the party, they must locate their other half.

### Come Find Your Long, Lost Love

Cupid's Valentine Gala
at Sarah and Fred's
Time, Date
RSVP: Telephone Number
DRESS: Casual Red

## Decorations, Flowers, and Name Tags

It's all hearts! Hearts hanging from the ceiling, heart-shaped balloons mixed with red and white balloons, and heart name tags. Mix hearts in with your centerpiece of red, pink, and white carnations or roses and baby's breath. String red and white twinkling lights for a festive atmosphere.

### Menu

Chicken Casserole
Tossed Green Salad
Crusty French Bread
Broiled Tomatoes
Strawberry Cake

# CHICKEN CASSEROLE

6 chicken breast halves
  Salt and pepper
  Paprika
3 bay leaves
1 stick of butter, softened

8 ounces sour cream
1 $10^3/_4$-ounce can cream of chicken soup
$1^1/_2$ cups crushed Ritz® Crackers
2 tablespoons sesame seeds

Place chicken breasts in a casserole dish. Sprinkle with salt, pepper, paprika, and top with bay leaves. Add an inch of water. Cover and bake at 350° for one hour. Take meat off bones and cut into bite-size chunks. Mix sour cream and soup and then chicken. Place in casserole dish. In a small saucepan melt butter and add sesame seeds and then Ritz Cracker crumbs. Spread cracker mixture on top of chicken. Can be made ahead and refrigerated overnight. Bake at 325° for 30 minutes and serve hot.

# STRAWBERRY CAKE

1 package white cake mix
1 3-ounce package strawberry Jello
$3/_4$ cup vegetable oil

4 eggs
1 cup frozen strawberries, drained

Beat all ingredients together. Bake in two heart-shaped pans or two square cake pans at 350° for 25 minutes.

# STRAWBERRY ICING

1 stick butter
$1/_2$ cup strawberries, drained

1 16-ounce box confectioners' sugar

Using a hand-mixer, mix butter and sugar until smooth. Add berries. Add more sugar to make icing thicker, if needed. Frost cake. Garnish with fresh strawberries and whipped cream.

# Fourth of July Cookout

The *lighted* candle is one of *life's* most
*extravagant* displays.
ANN PLATZ

Americans love to celebrate our heritage and independence on the Fourth
of July with parades, fireworks displays, and, especially, backyard picnics.
Invite your friends and family over for a cookout. You supply the drinks,
the hamburgers and hot-dogs with fixings, and assign each guest a dish to
complete the meal.

## Invitations

For easy invitations, use red, white, and blue stationery. You can also purchase
a variety of Fourth of July invitations. For those of you who would like to
try something elaborate, cover a cardboard tube in red crepe paper and
fringe it with blue and white crepe paper at the bottom. Roll up a written
or printed invitation and place it inside the tube with a long string
attached to a note that says "pull." Fill the tube with red, white, and blue
confetti and enclose it with more red crepe paper. Mail it to your guests in
a larger tube that can be purchased at the post office or made from another
cardboard tube reinforced with masking tape.

Celebrate the Fourth of July
with a Bang!
The Hueys' Backyard Cookout
Date, Time, and Place

Please Bring ————————————
RSVP: Telephone Number      Attire: Casual

## Decorations and Flowers

Fly American flags throughout the back and front yards. Tie red, white, and blue balloons to the lamppost and the trees. String red, white, and blue lights to brighten the party when darkness falls. Cover your tables with red, white, and blue tablecloths. For each individual table, fill glass containers with apples to hold red, white, and blue flowers and a miniature flag. Serve the food from platters and baskets tied with red, white, and blue bows. Use a drum container for serving a special dish trimmed in red, white, and blue.

## Music

This is the perfect day to crank up the stereo with the "Star Spangled Banner," favorite marches, and patriotic tunes such as "Yankee Doodle," "America the Beautiful," and John Philip Sousa marches.

## Menu

*Hot Dogs and Hamburgers
with All the Trimmings
Shish Kebabs
Potato Salad
Cole Slaw
Baked Beans
Flag Cake
Watermelon*

## FLAG CAKE

*Serves 14*

2 pints strawberries
1 loaf Sara Lee® Pound Cake

1½ cups blueberries
1 8-ounce container Cool Whip®

Line the bottom of an 8 x 12 baking dish with pound cake slices. Top with 1 cup sliced strawberries and 1 cup blueberries. Save remaining fruit. Spread Cool Whip® over cake and fruit. Slice remaining strawberries into halves and, along with remaining blueberries, place over whipped topping to make a flag design. Refrigerate until ready to serve.

# Trim-the-Tree Party

*Christmas!* No other time grants us, quite, this *vision*—
round the *tree* or gathered before the *fire*,
we *perceive* anew, with *joy*, one another's faces.

ELIZABETH BOWEN

Just after Thanksgiving, inspire your family and friends to get in the Christmas spirit. Invite people of all ages over to your home for a Trim-the-Tree Party to kick off the holiday! Have them drop by in the afternoon and stay for a light supper, caroling, and then dessert!

## Invitations

This is such a busy time of the year, so be sure to send your invitations out at least two weeks in advance. Trace a Christmas tree on heavy green construction paper and cut it out. Write your invitations with a red pen on the tree. Glue red hot candies at the tip of each branch and affix a silver star to the top of the tree. For a variation, you can use all silver stars or sequins and glitter. For easier invitations, write on red or green paper.

Bring an ornament
**To Trim-the-Tree**
Gather at Suzy and Stanley Daniels'
Light Supper
From four until nine
RSVP: Telephone Number   Dress: Casual

## Decorations

Line your walkway with luminarias. Mexican in origin, these are brown, white, or colored paper bags with cutouts. Fill the bag halfway with sand. Anchor a votive candle in the sand. Light luminarias and candles throughout the house just before your guests arrive. Hang a festive wreath on your front door and outline the door frame with fresh evergreen garlands. String tiny glittering lights on the trees.

Inside, hang your stockings with care on the mantle decked with pine boughs, apples, lemons, oranges, and pineapples with candles flickering in hurricane globes at each end. Light a fire in the fireplace. For colorful flames, sprinkle the logs with copper sulfate (it can be purchased from your druggist). Also, toss lemon and orange rinds, fresh evergreens, cloves, and cinnamon sticks in the fire for a Christmas fragrance to permeate the room. A pot of oranges spiked with cinnamon and cloves boiling on the stove will send a spicy aroma floating throughout the house.

Cover the dining room table with a Christmas cloth topped with red candles and a centerpiece of fragrant apples, pineapples, and greenery. Nearby on the buffet or sideboard are two punch bowls encircled with sprigs of holly with red berries. Tie punch ladles with a red bow and sprig of holly. Trays and bowls of Christmas treats are placed throughout the entertaining area. The guests help themselves to eggnog or punch and then mingle throughout the rooms.

As lights are already on the Christmas tree, invite the guests to join the *elves* in hanging the ornaments. Encourage your guests to make the ornament that they bring. Set up Santa's workshop for the children and include the supplies for making ornaments. Appoint a teen-age family member or friend as a Santa's helper to supervise the production of ornaments. At the end of the evening give prizes to all the children and the adult with the most original ornament.

After about an hour, when the tree is decked out in all its finery, the guests are invited to the dining room buffet for a light supper. The children stay in their own area for their special Christmas treats: Pigs in a blanket, carrot sticks, pear salad, and cookies.

After supper, invite your guests, including the children, to go caroling outdoors or to gather around the piano to sing. (The fireplace works if there is no piano!) Make copies of carols for all the guests. Assorted Christmas cookies and cakes are laid out on the dining room table and the guests fill their cups with steaming apple cider and hot chocolate. The party comes to a close as the hosts bid "Merry Christmas to all, and to all a goodnight!"

## *Music*

Play a variety of Christmas carols softly in the background. To end the evening, sing "Silent Night."

## *Menu*

Eggnog
Wassail Bowl
Green and Red Apples with Dip
Orange Glazed Pecans and Toffee
Tea Sandwiches
Pecan-Cheddar Wreath filled with Strawberry Preserves
Soup
Crusty French Bread
A Wreath of Christmas Cookies
Plate of Assorted Slices of Christmas Cakes

# WORLD'S BEST EGGNOG

1 quart thick eggnog, whipped
  to 2 quarts
1 quart regular eggnog
2 quarts vanilla ice cream, softened

2 Tablespoons rum flavoring
  nutmeg

Combine all ingredients except ice cream. Before serving mix in ice cream using an electric mixer. Serve in punch cups and sprinkle with nutmeg. (If you can't find thick eggnog, use 3 quarts regular eggnog.)

# PECAN-CHEDDAR CHRISTMAS WREATH

1 pound sharp cheddar cheese,
  grated
1 cup chopped pecans
3/4 cup mayonnaise

1 medium onion, grated
1 clove garlic, pressed
1/2 teaspoon Tabasco® sauce
1 cup strawberry preserves

Combine all ingredients except preserves. Mix well. Chill and then mold into a ring. Chill again and, when ready to serve, fill the center with strawberry preserves. Serve with crackers.

### HOW TO ASSEMBLE COOKIE WREATH

Stack cookies three cookies high and arrange in a circle. Add bow.

# CHOCOLATE TOFFEE

2 sticks butter
1 cup sugar

1 6-ounce package chocolate chips
1 cup chopped pecans

Line a 9 x 13 pan with waxed paper. Sprinkle bottom with ⅓ cup pecans which have been chopped coarsely. Put butter and sugar in saucepan over medium heat. Stir constantly with wooden spoon until candy reaches the hard crack stage (300° on a candy thermometer). Mixture will begin to brown. Pour hot mixture over pecans. Layer chocolate chips over hot mixture, spreading evenly. (Chocolate will melt.) Add remaining nuts over top. Press into chocolate. Cool in refrigerator for two hours. Break into pieces.

# ORANGE GLAZED PECANS

4 cups pecan halves

1/2 cup frozen orange juice

1 1/2 cups sugar

1/4 teaspoon cinnamon

Place pecans on cookie sheet and bake for 10 minutes until toasted. Bring juice concentrate, sugar, and cinnamon to a boil, stirring constantly. Remove from heat and stir in toasted pecans. Drop pecans onto foil-lined baking sheet and let stand until firm.

# 8

## Making Each Day Special

Gather ye *rosebuds* while ye may,
Old Time is still a-*flying*!

ROBERT HERRICK

*M*ost of us treasure the time we spend with family and friends during the holidays, but we often forget to celebrate the ordinary days of our lives. Make a memory for all those around you and especially for those you love!

Small gestures say "I love and care about you in a big way!" It's the simple pleasures of life that build our self-esteem. A heart-shaped sandwich tucked in your child's lunch box or a love note in your spouse's briefcase or a cup of coffee with a hurting friend can work miracles! Remember the words of Grandma Moses: "Life is what you make it!"

Perhaps Johnny brought home a good report card, Maggie lost a tooth, Michael hit a home run, or Sarah made a soccer goal. Light the candles! Celebrate! Every time I (Susan) visit my four-year-old godson Will, he tells his mother, "Aunt Suzy's here, let's have a party table!" His mother lights the candles for dinner and he and sister Lily can hardly wait to blow out the candles after we eat!

For that special someone in your life, schedule a date for just the two of you. Cook his favorite foods, plan a breakfast in bed, or take a walk hand-in-hand to watch the setting sun. Back rubs after a stressful day are greatly appreciated. When you're away from home, a love sonnet left behind on a pillow or a good night call can make one's spirits soar.

# Breakfast in Bed

There are two ways of *spreading* light: to be
The *candle* or the mirror that *reflects* it.

EDITH WHARTON

Whip up a tray of affection as you serve breakfast in bed to those you love, and make it luxurious, thoughtful, and delicious. There's no finer smell anywhere than the aroma of fresh-made coffee filling the morning air. This tray of delights should include favorite foods, but don't forget the morning devotional, newspaper, linen napkins, bud vase with a favorite bloom, smiling photograph, and a handwritten thought or verse to show you care.

Breakfast with your spouse can be a most intimate and inspiring meal as the two of you make plans for the day together. What better way to lavish attention on the one you love for a special anniversary, birthday, or just to say, "I love you." Open the shades and let the sun shine in!

## Details

Prepare the tray as much as possible the night before. If you can, set your coffee on a timer. Line a tray with a cloth or paper place mat and set with your finest china and silverware. Arrange all the items needed for your menu on the tray—cream and sugar servers, butter, preserves, jams, salt, and pepper.

## Menu

Fresh Squeezed Orange Juice in a Chilled Glass
French Toast with Berries and Syrup
Hash Brown Casserole
Coffee

99

# HASH BROWN CASSEROLE

1 2-pound package frozen
  hash browns
1 10³/₄-ounce can cream of chicken
  soup

8 slices bacon
1 8-ounce carton sour cream
3 cups shredded cheddar cheese
1 medium onion, chopped

Cook bacon and drain on a paper towel. Saute onion in bacon grease. Crumble 6 slices of bacon and mix with onion, chicken soup, sour cream, hash browns, and all except one cup of the shredded cheese. Pour into a 9 x 13 baking dish. Top with remaining cheese and bake at 350° for 45-60 minutes until golden brown. Garnish with remaining bacon before serving. This can be made ahead.

# ORANGE FRENCH TOAST

2 eggs
¹/₂ teaspoon salt
1 cup orange juice
1 cup fine bread crumbs

1 tablespoon orange peel
6 slices sour dough bread
4 tablespoons butter

In a mixing bowl, combine eggs, salt, and orange juice. Mix bread crumbs and orange peel together in separate bowl. Dip bread into egg mixture, then into crumbs. Melt butter in skillet over low heat and brown each side of the toast. Serve hot with syrup and fresh fruit.

# Mother-Daughter-Doll
## Tea Party

Each chair holds *memories* dear
Of *those* gathered 'round
Our *table*
*Through* the years.

SUSAN WALES

This wonderful party will gather mothers and daughters together. If there are friends without daughters, ask them to bring a friend that's like a daughter. It's always special to get dressed up in your finery. This is a great opportunity for the college set to get together for a school break and also a great time for little girls to bring along their favorite doll. The hostess and her daughter pour at a small tea, but for a larger event, two friends are invited to do the honors.

## Invitations

If you don't buy your invitations, make them in the shape of a tea pot or use plain paper with a contrasting pen.

Mrs. Mary Ellen Hansen and Miss Lily Hansen
invite you to join them for a
### Mother-Daughter Tea
Date and Time
Bring your favorite doll
RSVP: Telephone Number    DRESS: Party Clothes

## Decorations, Flowers, and Name Tags

Just decorate your table with a couple of dolls or add a fresh centerpiece of roses and greenery in a china teapot on your table overlaid with a white or ivory tablecloth. You can be creative with the name tags and make them in the shape of a teacup, but it's just as easy to buy teacup stickers to attach a name tag. Set up a small table for the girls' dolls with a tea set.

*Music*

Have a pianist play music softly or play a CD or tape throughout the afternoon.

## *Menu*

Assortment of Teas with Sugar and Cream
Lemons, Limes, Oranges
Strawberries Drizzled with White and Dark Chocolate
Assorted Tea Sandwiches Cut into Heart or Oval Shapes
Cucumber, Salmon, Egg Salad, and Watercress Sandwiches
Orange-Cranberry Scones with Preserves and Jams
Cheese Straws
Assorted Cookies and Jam Cake

## ORANGE-CRANBERRY SCONES

*Makes 8 scones*

| | |
|---|---|
| 2 cups all-purpose flour | 2 eggs |
| 2 teaspoons baking powder | 1/2 teaspoon salt |
| 1/2 stick of butter | 1/3 cup whipping cream |
| 1/2 cup coarsely grated orange peel | 1 cup Craisins™ |

Combine flour, baking powder, and salt in a large mixing bowl. Work butter into mixture with fork until it resembles meal. Mix in one egg at a time and then add cream, orange peel, and Craisins™. Knead dough on lightly floured surface until smooth. Roll out the dough about 3/4" thick. Use a 3" inch round cookie cutter to cut out scones. Place them on a baking sheet and bake at 425° for 20 minutes.

Can be prepared ahead.

# EGG SALAD

*Makes 12 round sandwiches or 6 regular sandwiches*

4 hard-boiled eggs

8 stuffed olives, sliced

8 slices cooked bacon, crumbled

1 tablespoon grated onion

1 tablespoon chopped chives

1/2 cup sour cream

2 tablespoons lemon juice

1 tablespoon mayonnaise

1 teaspoon salt

1 teaspoon pepper

1 teaspoon paprika

Break eggs with fork and add olives, bacon, onions, and chives. Combine remaining ingredients and add to egg mixture. Top or fill sandwiches.

# Romantic Candlelight Dinner for Two

Shut the *door*, not that it lets in the *cold*,
But that it lets out the *coziness*.

MARK TWAIN

Every married couple should plan a date night for just the two of you. On occasion, send the kids to spend the night with friends or grandparents and have a romantic evening in your own home so you can serve your husband a delicious dinner of all his favorite foods and create an atmosphere of love!

One of the greatest elements of a romantic evening is anticipation. Invite your husband to dinner in advance by leaving a note on his pillow at least a week before your evening. Then call him at least once during the day telling him: "It's only four more hours till I see you!"

Set the table with your finest linens, china, silver, and crystal. Choose a dress in his favorite color. Just before he arrives, dim the lights, light the candles, turn on soft music, spray the perfume, and get ready for love and romance.

Greet him at the door with a big kiss and a tray of hors d'oeuvres and invite him to relax in his favorite chair while you get dinner on the table.

## Decorations

Choose an arrangement of flowers that have a special significance to you, such as flowers from a rose bush your husband gave you or the flowers he usually sends you or perhaps flowers that you chose for your wedding bouquet. Use candles on each side of the arrangement. Arrange your food with color in mind and add garnishes.

*Menu*

Hot Artichoke Dip
Tossed Green Salad
Pork Tenderloin with Fruit
Green Beans with Almonds
Broiled Tomato
Calypso Pie

## PORK TENDERLOIN

*Serves 6-8*

| | |
|---|---|
| 3 pound pork tenderloin | ¹/₂ teaspoon ginger |
| 1 medium onion, sliced | ¹/₂ teaspoon dried mustard |
| 1 cup apricot preserves | |

Cover pork with onions and roast at 350° for 30 minutes. Mix remaining ingredients. Baste with glaze and cook another 30 minutes and glaze again. Test internal temperature with meat thermometer for 155-160°. Let roast stand 5 minutes. Serve with sauce.

## SAUCE

| | |
|---|---|
| 2 cups water | ¹/₂ cup walnuts |
| 1 Granny Smith (green tart apple) | ¹/₂ stick butter |
| 1 Rome Beauty apple (tart red apple) | 1 cup brown sugar |
| 1 12-ounce box prunes | |

Core and cut apples into 2″ pieces. Heat apples in water over medium heat. Add prunes and cook for 30 minutes. Add butter and brown sugar. Add walnuts and cook another 30 minutes. Serve hot with sliced pork tenderloin.

# CALYPSO PIE

*Serves 10*

18 Oreo® cookies, crushed
$^1/_3$ cup melted margarine
2 quarts coffee ice cream, softened
$1^1/_2$ ounces unsweetened chocolate
$^1/_2$ cup sugar

1 teaspoon margarine
1 $5^1/_3$-ounce can evaporated milk
1 pint whipping cream, whipped
$^1/_2$ cup pecans, chopped

Mix crushed cookies with $^1/_3$ cup melted margarine. Press into bottom of a 9 x 13 pan. Freeze. Spread softened ice cream evenly over crust. Return to freezer. Combine chocolate, sugar, 1 teaspoon margarine, and milk in heavy saucepan. Cook until thick. Cool. Pour over ice cream. Cover top with whipped cream and sprinkle with pecans.

# The Party's Over

*The fragrance always remains in the
hand that gives the rose.*

HEDA BEJAR

## Farewell and Cleanup

Congratulations! You have just given a great gift to your guests—a good time and very special memories. The party's coming to a close. As each guest leaves, they are taking with them a little piece of your heart. But your hostess duties are far from over—there's still plenty to be done!

The hosts should excuse themselves from their other guests and see departing guests to the door. Tell each guest good-bye warmly and that you look forward to seeing them again soon. If they brought a dish, make sure their container is washed and returned. If there are party favors, make sure each guest has theirs. Your kindness and hospitality will be long remembered even after the details of the evening have grown dim.

As hosts of the event, you should have a great feeling of satisfaction and this will spur you on to cleanup! You and your husband can enjoy reminiscing over the events of the evening as you perform your kitchen duties.

## Cleanup Tips

Now comes the fun part—cleanup! Just kidding, but we do have some helpful hints that will assist you.

## Clearing the Table

+ Clear the dirty dishes and utensils between the courses.
+ Wait until all the guests are finished eating to clear the table. Always ask since guests sometimes take a momentary break from eating.
+ Always serve your guests from the left and remove the dishes from the right.

- Do not stack plates as you remove them.
- Make sure your counters are clear so you have a place to put the dishes.
- If you serve buffet and do not have a server to collect the plates, set up a separate table for guests to drop off their plates and a trash can for their disposable items.

## Cleaning

- Use a soft cloth or sponge, not a brush or abrasive pad that will scratch plates, to remove food from the plates.
- Have a large trash bag in your kitchen for throwing out food.
- Fill your sink with warm soapy water to soak the dishes. Have a separate container for silverware to soak.
- To remove tea or coffee stains from china, make a baking soda paste.
- Sprinkle burned pots with baking soda and add warm water. Simmer on stove for about ten minutes and then let soak for a few hours. Burned residue will pop right out.
- Re-season your pot or pan with olive oil.

## Hand Washing

- Hand wash fine china and crystal and any items with silver or gold rims. The high heat in the dishwasher will cause the rims to flake.
- Line your sink with rubber dividers and mats to avoid breaking and chipping your china and glass wear. If you don't have mats, use a soft towel.
- Wash fine china and crystal one piece at a time in the sink to avoid chipping.
- Add 1/2 cup of ammonia to your dishwater to remove film from crystal and china, but rinse thoroughly.
- When rinsing crystal, add one cup of vinegar to a sink of warm water.
- When drying fine crystal, do not rub with a towel because this could snap the glass.

# Dishwasher

- Add a cup of vinegar in a bowl in the bottom of your dishwasher to remove film from your glasses. Do not use with silver or aluminum—only glassware.

- Do not put knives or other silver with handles in dishwasher. Heat will cause them to separate.

- Never allow silver and stainless eating utensils to touch in a dishwasher. It will cause spots on the silver.

- When loading your silverware in the dishwasher, group your spoons, knives, forks—this will save time unloading.

- To remove odors from your dishwasher, place a bowl of baking soda in the bottom of the dishwasher. Sprinkle 2 tablespoons of baking soda in the bottom of the dishwasher. Close the dishwasher and allow soda to stand overnight. The next morning remove bowl, but leave remaining baking soda in bottom of dishwasher. Odors will be gone!

# Storage
## CHINA

- Use paper plates or napkins or purchase plate dividers to put between your plates for protection from breaking and scratches.

- Only stack plates of the same size.

## CRYSTAL

• Always store your crystal upright as it appears on your table. The stem is made for standing, but the rim of the glass is more delicate.

## SILVER

• Make sure silver is dry before you put it away or it will rust.

• Never store silver wrapped in newspaper or use rubber bands. They will damage or spot silver. Also do not use rubber gloves when polishing silver for this same reason.

• Place a piece of chalk in your silver chest. It prevents tarnish—really!

• Wrap your silver in silver cloth for ultimate protection.

## *Leftovers*

• It is usually not advisable to keep leftovers longer than four days, but they can be frozen. Be sure to mark your frozen items with contents and date. If you have a surplus of leftovers, you may want to send some home with your guests.

Now that your work is done, take a few minutes to relax with your husband as the fire's last embers burn away before you say goodnight! This is the sweetest possible ending to a perfect evening!

## *The Entertaining Journal*

Keep a notebook or buy an entertaining journal to keep a record of your guests, the menu, and your recipes. You can use the entertaining book as a guide to another evening and it also makes a nice family heirloom and memory book. This would make a wonderful gift to a daughter one day to use as her entertaining guide and will provide her with your best recipes. In earlier days, cookbooks were a woman's diary and a record of her life. Women kept home remedies and mementos as well as recipes in their books. Cookbooks and cooking journals were the first books ever published by women in this country. Start a special heirloom for your family!

# Thanks for the Memories

Another special family custom you can include is one my husband Ken's mother, Clara Ferree Smith, shared with me (Susan). Every time she and her husband, Dr. Wales Smith, a minister, entertained, she had each guest sign the tablecloth. Following the evening, she would then embroider their signature with a fine linen thread. They entertained celebrities and leaders in their denomination, and today the tablecloth is proudly displayed in the museum at the church's headquarters. Clara also believed that every guest that left her home should leave with a memento. She made paper boxes with special verses personalized for each guest. You can begin these special traditions for your own family.

In closing, we would like to thank you for coming along with us on our entertaining journey! We know that you will be a great hostess and a blessing to all who enter your home.

> Blest be that *spot,* where cheerful guests *retire*
> To pause from *toil* and trim their evening *fire!*
> Blest that *abode* where want and pain *repair*
> And every *stranger* finds a ready *chair!*
>
> OLIVER GOLDSMITH